CONVERSE® ALL STAR™
BASKETBALL
HOW TO PLAY LIKE A PRO

A MOUNTAIN LION BOOK

John Wiley & Sons, Inc.
New York • Chichester • Brisbane • Toronto • Singapore

This text is printed on acid-free paper.

Copyright © 1996 by Mountain Lion, Inc.
Published by John Wiley & Sons, Inc.

The publisher and the author have made every reasonable effort to insure that the activities in the book are safe when conducted as instructed but assume no responsibility for any damage caused or sustained while performing the activities in this book. Parents, guardians, and/or coaches should supervise young readers who undertake the activities in this book.

Library of Congress Cataloging-in-Publication Data:

Converse all star basketball : how to play like a pro.
      p.   cm. — (Converse all star sports series)
   Includes index.
   ISBN 0-471-15977-8 (pbk. : alk. paper)
   1. Basketball—Handbooks, manuals, etc.   2. Basketball players—United States—Interviews. I. Converse (Firm) II. Series.
   GV885.C596   1996
   796.323'2—dc20   96-21551

Printed in the United States of America
10 9 8 7 6 5 4 3 2

CONTENTS

INTRODUCTION

From Peach Baskets to the NBA

It was the winter of 1891, and in Springfield, Massachusetts, the YMCA had a problem. It was too cold for football or baseball, and the athletes were bored with the same old indoor games. Dr. James Naismith, a gym instructor, invented a new game that would keep his students busy and having fun. He borrowed the idea of having goals at each end of the playing area from football, but his goals had to be smaller in order to work inside the gym. He decided to use a large, round ball that would be shot into the goals. He made up a list of thirteen rules. For the first game, he used a soccer ball, and for the goals, he found some empty peach baskets that he hung, high on the walls, at each end of the gym. That's how the game came to be known as basketball.

Naismith's students loved the game, even though there were some problems at first. Naismith left the bottoms in the baskets, so every time a player made a goal, someone had to climb up a ladder to get the ball back! Basketball became a big hit in Springfield. YMCA's all across the country adopted the game.

Basketball soon spread to other countries. By 1913, the rules were printed in 30 different languages. Basketball has been an Olympic event for men since 1936 and for women since 1972. Basketball became a nationally recognized professional sport in 1949 when the NBA (National Basketball Association) was formed. As the popularity of the game grew, some of the old rules were changed and new ones were added. The three-point play was introduced for both professionals and amateurs and the shot clock was instituted at the professional and collegiate levels to speed up the game and to provide for more scoring.

Today basketball is one of the most popular sports in the world, and especially in the United States. The NCAA (National Collegiate Athletic Association) sponsors its "March Madness"—a 64-team, single-elimination tournament that captures our attention over three weekends of play early each spring. At the same time, the NCAA conducts the Women's Basketball Tournament which also features 64 teams competing to be crowned as National Champions. Thirty-two other collegiate teams vie for the NIT (National Invitational Tournament) title and eight other women's teams play to determine the NWIT (National Invitational Women's Tournament) champion. The NBA follows later in the spring with its play-off games which concludes with a final best-of-seven games series in June.

Throwing a basketball at the hoop is easy. But shooting the ball takes a lot of know-how and practice. The chapters in this book teach you how to handle the ball, how to pass, and how to shoot. You'll find coaching tips plus advice from basketball pro Kevin Johnson, and drills that will make you a better player. Each chapter ends with games that you can play with your friends, because if you want to play like a pro, you've got to practice like one. Share this book with your friends and family. They'll want to play like pros, too!

In order to keep the instructions in this book as simple as possible, the word "he" is used to mean either boys or girls.

To make the instructions as interesting as possible, we have included bits of information and trivia concerning various players, coaches and teams in the history of basketball. Their inclusion is not an indication of an endorsement of any product, but to enhance your enjoyment and learning experience.

CHAPTER 1

This Game Called Basketball

Basketball is a fast-moving sport. The players move the ball from one goal to the other and back again, in a matter of seconds. They sprint, leap, pass, and shoot, with arms and legs flying. When you're watching basketball, you're on the edge of your seat. When you're *playing* basketball then it's you, making the excitement. If you love the game and want to play, that's a good start. But you also need to practice, practice, practice.

Getting Started

Before you can play basketball, you need to know a little about the game.

The Aim of the Game

Two teams of five players each try to *shoot* (throw) the ball into the basket (the goal) to score points. While one team has the ball, the other team tries to stop them from scoring points. The team with the most points at the end of the game is the winner.

Get the Team Spirit!

Basketball players are a part of a *team*. Five players have to work together to make the most goals they can for their team. To keep the team spirit you have to play for the good of your team, instead of trying to be a superstar.

The Basketball

The ball is round, and its size is between 29½ inches and 30 inches around its middle. The ball is orange, and has a grainy texture. It's filled with air that's under pressure, just like in a bicycle tire. That's so the ball will bounce when dropped.

The NBA and the NCAA

The NBA is the National Basketball Association. This is the major league of teams in the United States. NBA players are professionals, or *pros*.

The NCAA is the National Collegiate Athletic Association. It is the group that makes the rules for college basketball.

The Court

The basketball *court* is a rectangle. The court used by the NBA is 50-feet wide and 94-feet long. In high school, the court is usually 84-feet long. In youth league, the court may be smaller, depending on the size of the gym.

The lines around the outside of the rectangle are called the *sidelines* and the *baselines*. There needs to be at least 3 feet of clear space around the outside of the sidelines and end lines, so players won't run into anything if they go out-of-bounds (cross the sidelines or end lines) during play.

The court is divided across the middle by the *midcourt* line. The midcourt line divides the court into the *front court* and the *backcourt*.

The front court is the half of the court with the basket that your team shoots for. Your team's back court is the half of the court with the basket that the other team shoots for. Your team's backcourt is the other team's front court.

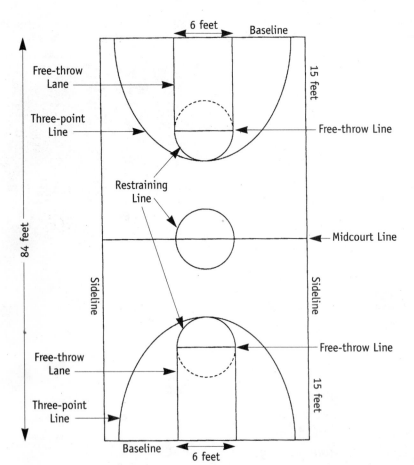

6 feet — Baseline — 15 feet — Free-throw Lane — Three-point Line — Free-throw Line — Restraining Line — Midcourt Line — 84 feet — Sideline — Sideline — Free-throw Lane — Free-throw Line — Three-point Line — 15 feet — Baseline — 6 feet

At the center of the midcourt line are two circles, one inside the other. The smaller circle is called the *center circle* and the bigger one is the *jump circle*. The game starts inside the restraining circle with a jump ball. There will be more about the jump ball later in this chapter.

The Baskets

At each end of the court is a goal, or *basket*. The basket has a *hoop* (round, metal ring) that is 18 inches across with a net hanging from it. The basket is usually 10 feet from the floor, but youth leagues may use lower baskets. The hoop is attached to a *backboard*. The backboard is flat and is usually painted white or made of clear glass.

The *three-point line* is a large half-circle that is drawn on the floor around each basket. Any goals made from outside this line count for three points.

The *free-throw line* is a line drawn on the floor that is 15 feet out in front of the backboard. The lines drawn from the ends of the free throw line to the end line mark off an area called the *free-throw lane*. The free throw lane is also called the *key*.

Scoring

When you shoot the ball into the basket (Figure 1-1), and it either stays in the basket or passes through it, then you've made a *shot* (scored a goal). Shots may be made from anywhere on the court. Successful shots are also called *field goals*, with the exception of a *free throw*. A free throw is when the player shoots from the free-throw line (also known as the foul line) without interference from the other team.

A field goal that was shot from behind the three-point line is worth three points.

A free throw is worth one point.

All other field goals are worth two points.

Equipment

You don't really need a lot of special equipment to play basketball. Since the game doesn't have a lot of physical contact (like tackling in football), you don't need pads or helmets. If you are playing on a school team, then you will be wearing a uniform in your school colors with your player number on your chest and back.

To play basketball in gym class or with your friends, wear lightweight clothes such as shorts and a tank top. Because basketball means a lot of running with quick starts and stops, it is very important to wear a pair of good-fitting, rubber-soled shoes, such as court shoes, or running shoes.

1-1 SHOOTING: The only way to score in the game of basketball is to shoot the ball into the basket. Many teams play great defense, others have great passing, but in order to win games, you must shoot well.

Timing

The game is divided into time periods, but these time periods are different lengths for high school, college, and the pros. High school teams play four, eight-minute *quarters*. College teams play two, twenty-minute *halves*, and the NBA uses four, twelve-minute *quarters*.

Youth league uses four, six-minute quarters with a ten minute break between halves.

Extra time periods called *overtimes* are played when the score is tied at the end of the fourth quarter. If the score is still tied at the end of the overtime period, then another overtime is added until the tie is broken. An overtime period is three minutes.

Offense and Defense

When your team has the ball, then you are playing *offense*. While playing offense, your team's job is to shoot the ball into the basket and score points. When the other team has the ball, then your team is playing defense and your job is to keep the offensive players from scoring points, and to get the ball back for your team.

The Players

Each team has five players on the court at one time. Each of the five players has a position to play. There are three basic positions: guard, forward, and center. (Some coaches refer to the basic positions by different names such as post, wing, and point guard.)

- There are two **guards**. These are usually smaller, faster players, and good ball handlers. When your team has the ball, the guards bring it up the court. The guards are also good shooters. Guards can drive past the defenders (defensive players) to the basket, or they can pass the ball to a teammate.

- There are two **forwards**. The forwards handle the ball in the front court along the end line or out to the sides of the three-point goal line.

- The **center** is usually a taller player who plays inside the three-point line and close to the basket. The center is also called the post player (because he's close to the post that holds up the basket). The center starts the game for his team with a jump ball.

Outside the Lines

WOMEN'S BASKETBALL

Only a month after basketball was invented in 1891 at the YMCA in Springfield, Massachusetts, women began dropping in to practice. By 1893 Smith College had formed women's teams and held the first women's college game.

Lynette Woodard of Kansas averaged 26.3 points per game, captained the U.S. Olympic team to a gold medal in 1984, and she was the first woman to join the Harlem Globetrotters.

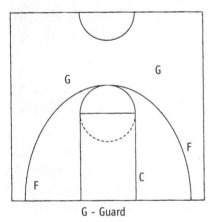

G - Guard
F - Forward
C - Center

Playing the Game

The Jump Ball

The game begins with a *jump ball*. The highest jumpers from each team (usually the centers) stand in the center of the court, inside the restraining circle. Their teammates are just outside the restraining circle. The referee tosses the ball up between the two jumpers, who leap into the air and try to bat the ball to a teammate.

Moving the Ball

Basketball players can move the ball by passing or by dribbling. Players *pass* by throwing the ball through the air to a teammate. They can also pass by bouncing the ball off the floor one time, toward their teammate.

Dribbling means bouncing the ball off the floor (Figure 1-2). To dribble, bounce the ball on the floor with one hand. When the ball comes back up to your hand, bounce it again. You may use either hand to dribble, but not both. You may switch hands while dribbling.

You can dribble while you are standing still or while you are running the ball up the court.

1-2 DRIBBLING: Dribbling is a vital part of the game. Besides passing, it's the only way to move the ball up the floor. Every good basketball player, regardless of size, possesses excellent dribbling skills.

The Body Obstacle Course Drill

Here's a drill to get you used to handling the basketball. Stand with your legs spread apart. You have to move the ball around your body without dropping the ball or letting it touch the floor (Figures 1-3 to 1-8).

1. *Move the ball in and out of your legs.*

2. *Pass the ball in a circle around your waist.*

3. *With your right hand, take the ball behind your back, then toss it forward over your left shoulder and catch it in front of you with your right hand again. Repeat with the left hand.*

4. *Hold both arms straight out in front of you. Quickly toss the basketball back and forth between your two hands. Keep tossing as you move your arms higher and higher, until they are straight up above your head. Keep tossing the ball back and forth as you bring your arms slowly back down again.*

See how long it takes you to do all four moves. Then see if you can do them faster the next time.

1-3 to 1-8 BODY OBSTACLE COURSE: Carry the ball through the legs from right to left, then back through from left to right. Flip the ball up behind the back to the opposite hand, then repeat the same step back the other way. Hold the ball out in front with both hands, tapping the ball back and forth. Slowly raise the arms above the head in the process and then back down to complete the drill.

The Rules

When a rule is broken, it's called a *violation*. Some of the most important rules of basketball include:

Guarding

Every player has the right to *guard* any part of the court if they get there before an opposing player. To guard an opponent means to stay close to him, and if he has the ball, try and steal it from him, or stop him from passing, or stop him from getting off a shot. But beware of committing a foul (see next page).

Traveling

You may move the ball by dribbling or passing, but you may not walk or run while holding the ball. If you do, it's called *traveling*. You may move one foot while holding the ball, but your other foot, or *pivot* foot, must stay in one place.

Alternating Possession

Whenever there is a held ball (two players on opposing teams both get their hands on the ball) or whenever two opposing players cause the ball to go out-of-bounds, then the rule of alternating possession tells the referee which team gets the ball. The rule of alternating possession means that the teams take turns getting the ball.

Out-of-Bounds

When a player touches the floor or any other object outside the sidelines or end lines, then he is out-of-bounds.

Putting the Ball Back in Play

After a basket is scored, or after a violation, or after the ball goes out-of-bounds, it is put back in play with a throw-in. The referee picks a spot out-of-bounds and gives the player the ball. The player has five seconds to throw the ball inbounds to a teammate.

Outside the Lines

THE TICKING CLOCK

In 1951, the Rochester Royals and the Indianapolis Olympians went into six overtimes and took four hours! No one wanted to shoot because they were afraid they'd lose the ball and the other team would score. The NBA now uses a shot clock so players have to shoot in twenty-four seconds.

There are other rules to make the game move faster:

• After a team has made a basket, the other team has five seconds to inbound the ball.

• After the ball is inbounded, the offense has ten seconds to get over the midcourt line.

• Offensive players can only stay in the free throw lane for three seconds.

How did you get started in basketball? At what age? What program?

I started by just shooting baskets with friends at the local parks in Sacramento, which later led to pick-up games. I started around the age of 11 or 12. The first real organized basketball program I participated in wasn't until high school. I did play on an informal junior high school team, but it really couldn't be considered a program.

Who had the greatest personal influence in your development?

The person who had the greatest influence on me as a player was Coach McKenna at Sacramento High School.

What advice would you give to a youngster starting out?

Be patient and practice hard. You can accomplish almost anything if you put the time in and work hard.

What is the first basketball lesson you would teach your son or daughter?

I would teach any youngster first starting out that basketball is a team game which requires all players to work together.

Do you get nervous before or during a game?

I sometimes get nervous before a game just thinking about it. When the game starts, however, I have a job to do so I am focused and don't have the time to get nervous.

Over and Back Violation

Your team must take the ball from the backcourt to the front court within ten seconds of taking possession of the ball. If your team has the ball in the front court, you can't take the ball back into the backcourt. If you do, it's called an *over and back violation*.

Fouls

There are two kinds of fouls: personal fouls and technical fouls.

1. **Personal Fouls.** Players are not allowed to hold, push, hit, or trip other players. If they do, it's a personal foul. If you foul an opponent while he's shooting, then the shooter is allowed two or three free throws, depending on whether it was going to be a two or a three point basket. If, however, the shooter still made the basket, then he gets only one free throw.

   When a personal foul is called, the ball is given to the other team or the other team may get one or more free throws, meaning that the player can shoot from the foul line without interference from the other team.

2. **Technical Fouls.** All fouls, except for personal fouls, are called technical fouls. Some technical fouls include: delaying the game by keeping the ball from going back into play, taking more than five time-outs, or having more than five players on the court at one time.

The Officials

There are two or three officials for a basketball game: a referee, and one or two umpires. They're out there on the court during the game making sure the rules are followed. If a rule is broken or a foul happens, an official blows a whistle to stop the game.

The Coach

The coach is really a teacher. His job is to teach his players how to play the game and show them how they can become better athletes. The coach plans the strategy for each game.

1-9 and 1-10 QUICK CATCH: Hold the ball between your legs with one arm in front of your legs and one behind. Quickly switch hands without allowing the ball to hit the ground.

Quick Catch Drill

Stand with your legs wide apart. With one hand in back of your legs and one hand in front, hold the basketball between your legs. Now switch hands. Don't let the basketball touch the floor. Your hands have to be lightning fast! (Figures 1-9 and 1-10)

Now hold the basketball in both hands in front of you. Bounce it backward between your legs and catch it behind you with both hands.

Getting in Shape for Basketball

Athletes need to be in top physical shape in order to have the strength and physical skills to do their jobs. Keeping fit helps protect you against getting hurt. A team whose players are in good shape will almost always beat an out-of-shape team.

Before playing basketball, or any other sport, you should always warm up your muscles by stretching them.

Regular exercise (three or four times a week) is also important to keep you fit for playing the game.

1-11 SKIER SQUAT: Squat straight down and slightly bend forward at the waist. You should feel the stretch in your thighs and calves.

1-12 UPPER LEG STRETCH: Standing, grab one leg and pull it up so the heel touches the rear end. Maintain balance with the other leg, then switch.

Always warm up before playing or practicing. Take a few laps around the court, then stretch your whole body (Figures 1-11 and 1-12).

• **Legs.** Pick up one foot and move your ankle in a circle. Then do the same with the other ankle. Now keep your feet together and flat on the floor. Keeping your knees straight, bend over from your waist and try to grab your toes. Don't stretch farther than is comfortable. Hold this position for ten seconds, then straighten up. Repeat three times.

• **Waist.** Stand with your feet a shoulder's width apart. Put one hand on your hip and raise your other arm straight up above your head and make a fist. Bend your body (at the waist) to the side away from your raised arm. You'll feel the stretch in your side. Don't stretch farther than is comfortable. Reverse your arms and stretch to the other side. Repeat several times.

• **Arms and Shoulders.** Raise one arm straight above your head. Bend the elbow so that your hand is resting on the back of your neck. Grab your elbow with your other hand, and gently push down. Don't stretch farther than is comfortable. Now switch arms and stretch the other side.

Exercises that you can do on your own to stay in shape include: jogging, sprinting (running fast for a short distance), making quick turns while sprinting, jumping rope, and climbing up and down stairs.

Sometimes, basketball players work out with weights. Young players under the age of fourteen probably shouldn't lift weights

1-13 LINE LEAPS: Stand with both feet together on one side of a straight line. leap in the air (keeping both feet together) across to the other side of the line and continue to do so for 30 seconds, back and forth.

1-14 SKI TUCKS: Stand with both feet together, jump straight up in the air, and bring your knees into your chest. Try to get as high as the player in the picture.

Jumping Drill

Since jumping is important in basketball, here's a drill to help you jump higher. Stand next to a wall with a piece of chalk in your hand. Hold it up high and leap into the air, making a chalk mark as high up on the wall as you can get (Figure 1-15). Now do ten more jumps and make sure that each one is at least as high as your chalk mark. (Make sure that you're wearing your court shoes and that you practice someplace where the chalk mark won't matter. Don't try this on the side of the house or the neighbor's garage.)

1-15 JUMPING DRILL: Stand up against a wall, jump straight up in the air and touch the highest point on the wall possible.

1-16 INNER THIGH STRETCH: Standing, spread your legs out and shift your weight over to one side. Bend down so that your chest is leaning against your thigh, but keep the opposite side leg straight. Hold it for ten seconds and switch.

1-17 PRETZEL: Sit down on the floor wih your left leg straight out in front. Place your right leg over your left leg with the knee bent. Press your left elbow against the knee of your right leg and turn your upper body to the right. Do the same stretch for the opposite side.

1-18 and 1-19 ARM STRETCHES: In the first stretch above, grab your arm by the tricep muscle and pull it across your chest until a

stretch is felt. For the second stretch (right), reach straight back with one arm over your shoulder and behind your head. Grab your elbow with the other arm and pull back. Each of these exercises should be done several times with each arm.

1-20 BUTTERFLY: Sit on the floor and bring both heels together. Press down on the inside of both knees with your elbows and pull both feet in toward your body. This is the best way to stretch out the groin muscles.

1-21 HIP FLEXOR STRETCH: Get into a sprinter's position (both hands on the floor, one leg bent in toward your chest and leaning forward) extend one leg back and push the hip to the ground. This stretches the upper thigh and trunk regions. Make sure to stretch both sides.

1-22 ACHILLES STRETCH: Get horizontal to the ground and support yourself with your arms and one leg. Put your right foot over and slightly behind your left and put the weight of your body on the foot on the ground. After ten seconds, switch legs. You should feel the stretch just below your calf.

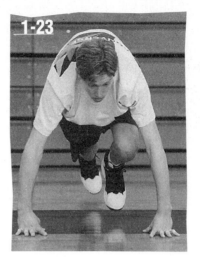

1-23 MOUNTAIN CLIMBERS: Get into the sprinter's position with your right leg extended back. Interchange the leg positions back and forth, simulating a climbing motion.

Make It Up, Play It Out

Here's a game that you can play all by yourself to learn how to aim for the basket.

Ghostball

You need a ball and a hoop on a backboard for this game. Pretend there is a ghost sitting on top of the basket. Every time you get the ball past the ghost (into the basket), you get two points. Every time the ghost gets the ball (you miss), the ghost gets one point. The first one to get 200 points is the winner.

Outside the Lines

THE OUTER LIMITS

According to the Official NBA Encyclopedia, the tallest player on record is 7 ft. 7 in. and the shortest player is 5 ft. 3 in.

TALLEST: 7 ft. 7 in. Manute Bol, Gheorge Muresan; 7 ft. 6 in. Shawn Bradley; 7 ft. 5 in. Chuck Nevitt; 7 ft. 4 in. Mark Eaton, Ralph Sampson, Rik Smits

SHORTEST: 5 ft. 3 in. Muggsy Bogues; 5 ft. 7 in. Gregg Grant, Red Klotz, Wat Misaka, Monte Towe, Spud Webb

CHAPTER 2

Dribbling

Dribbling is the way you can move the ball up the court without passing. Dribbling means bouncing the ball off the floor with your hand. You may use either hand to dribble, but not both. You may switch hands while dribbling.

When you are dribbling the ball, you are in *possession* of it. For each possession of the ball, you are allowed only one non-stop stretch of dribbling. Once you stop dribbling and pick up the ball, you have used up your dribble and you must pass or shoot the ball. If you pass the ball to your teammate and he passes it back to you, you are allowed another stretch of dribbling.

Dribbling is a very important ball handling skill and all players need to become experts at dribbling.

How to Dribble

Dribbling looks easy, but it takes many hours of practice in order to become an expert. Here are the basics of good dribbling:

1. **Spread your fingers wide.** You will cover more of the ball and have better control over it. Use your fingers to dribble the ball. Don't slap the ball with your palms.

2. **Keep your elbows and wrists loose and floppy.** This forces your hand and arm to move a little when the ball bounces back up to your hand. If your arm is stiff, you will find yourself slapping at the ball and you won't have it under control.

3. **Stay low to the ground.** Bend your knees and crouch over a bit. Staying low makes it easier to move around and gives you better control of the ball. Don't let the ball bounce too high. Keep it at waist level.

4. While dribbling in a game, **keep your body between your opponent and the ball.** Your body can help you protect the ball from the opponent.

5. **Keep your other arm out in front of you.** This will make it harder for the opponent to steal the ball.

6. **Keep your head up.** You have to know where your opponents are in order to protect the ball. Also, if you're looking down at the ball, you might miss a chance to score (Figure 2-1).

Left-Handed and Right-Handed Dribbling

Are you right-handed or left-handed? The hand you use to eat, to write, and to push the buttons on the telephone is your *dominant* hand. It's only natural that you'll want to dribble with your dominant hand, but don't fall into that trap!

If you dribble with one hand a lot more than the other, it will be easier for a defender to guard you, or steal the ball. He'll quickly learn from watching you that you dribble mostly with the one hand.

A good basketball player should be able to use both hands equally well. If you spend thirty minutes a day practicing dribbling with your dominant hand, then you should spend sixty minutes a day practicing with your other hand. Before you can move on to any fancy dribbling, make sure that you are comfortable dribbling with either hand.

Once you're good at dribbling with both hands, you're ready to learn some ways that you can use dribbling to fake (fool) the defender, so you can get in the clear to shoot.

2-1 DRIBBLING STANCE: Stay low to the ground and keep your body out in front of the ball. The nondribbling arm should also be extended to help protect the ball from the defensive player. Keep the head and eyes up to have good vision of the floor.

Switching Hands Drill

Dribble up the court with one hand and dribble back with the other. Then dribble up the court and back, changing hands on every bounce.

Blindfold Drill

Practice dribbling the ball while blindfolded. This will be very hard at first, but after a while, you'll begin to feel that the ball is a part of your hand and arm.

Fancy Dribbling

Crossover

In the *crossover* (Figures 2-2 and 2-3), you change hands while dribbling, then move quickly to shoot. Dribble on one side, while keeping your body between the ball and the defender. Turn your body slightly toward the defender, but stay between him and the ball. Look for an opening (area clear of defenders). When you see the opening, quickly switch hands to dribble on the other side, and drive (move) through the opening toward the basket. The defender won't be expecting this, and you should be able to get away from him to shoot.

The Rocker Step

The *rocker step* (Figures 2-4 to 2-7) is a fake step that fools the defender into thinking you are going to move one way, when you are really going to move in a different direction. The rocking motion of the step gives you momentum (power) for your direction change.

When you get the ball (before you start your dribble), hold it in both hands either above your head or to one side, away from the defender. (If you keep the ball in front of you, the defender will swipe at it.) Before you can *rock*, you need to *square up*, meaning that you have to pivot on one foot (plant one foot firmly on the floor and then spin on it) while bringing the other foot around so that you are facing, or almost facing, the defender. You want to pivot on the foot that's closest to the defender, and when you turn, swing your leg at him, so he will have to jump back in order to avoid fouling (making contact with) you.

Now that the defender is a little off balance, keep your pivot foot planted, and thrust your other foot toward him in a fake. The defender will most likely follow. As he does, bring that same leg back across your body and dribble in the other direction (toward the basket).

2-2 and 2-3 CROSSOVER DRIBBLE (for a right-handed dribble): First, dribble to the right of the defender, and then as you get to within a few feet of the player guarding you, cross your dribble over to your left hand and continue in that direction.

2-4 to 2-7 ROCKER STEP: Go to the right of the defender, stepping forward with your left foot. Then step back with the left foot, pivoting on your right foot, using a crossover dribble and continue to the defender's left.

Double Dribble Drill

Dribble two balls at the same time. Dribble one ball with your right hand and the other with your left. Dribble while standing still until you get the hang of it, then try dribbling around the court.

Through the Legs

Dribbling *through the legs* is one of the easier fancy dribbles, and the fans love watching this move (Figure 2-8).

To practice this move, stand with your legs apart with one leg out in front of the other. Start by dribbling the ball in front of you with the hand on the same side as your back leg. Bounce the ball behind your front leg to your other hand. Catch the ball and put it back in your other hand, then practice the dribble again. Do not bounce the ball back and forth behind your leg, because it's important to pass the ball behind your leg in the one direction only. After you've practiced several more dribbles, switch your legs, and practice some dribbles in the opposite direction. Always start the dribble with the hand on the same side as your back leg.

Now it's time to take this fancy dribble on the move. Start dribbling with your legs together. Now take a step forward with the leg opposite your dribbling hand. As you step forward, pass the ball behind that leg. As you step forward, the ball should bounce at the same time that your foot hits the ground. Stay low with your knees bent, because that will bring your passing hand closer to your receiving hand. Take a couple of steps in a row, dribbling the ball back and forth through your legs. Now speed up. With practice, you'll be good enough to do it in a game.

Behind the Back

Passing the ball *behind your back* (Figures 2-9 and 2-10) while dribbling can be a good move when you are being closely guarded by a defender. Move slowly toward the defender. Start your move by stepping forward with the foot opposite the hand that's controlling the ball. As you step forward, swing the ball behind your back and bounce it on the floor at an angle that will bring it up to your other hand, which will be reaching behind you to receive the ball. Immediately go into your dribble and move past the defender.

2-8 THROUGH THE LEGS: When dribbling with your right hand (as in this photo) step out with your left leg in front and then bounce the ball through your legs to your left hand. The quicker this can be accomplished, the more effective it is.

2-9 and 2-10 BEHIND THE BACK: Step forward with the foot on the dribbling side and bounce the ball around the back to the opposite hand. This move needs to be practiced in motion.

Change of Pace Dribble

Good dribbling always keeps your opponent off guard. If you dribble at the same tempo (speed) all the time, the person guarding you will be able to time his attack on the ball. If you don't want the ball stolen, you have to change the pace of (speed up and slow down) your dribble.

The most effective way to change pace is to dribble up to the defensive player with a slow, even dribble. Then, very suddenly, speed up. Don't pick up speed gradually, or the defender will be able to stay with you.

Going from a fast dribble to a slow one isn't used very often, but it can be helpful at certain times. If you are dribbling fast and the defender is sprinting along beside you, suddenly put on the brakes. The defender will tend to keep going and you'll be in the clear to take a shot.

Slalom Drill

Set up seven or eight chairs, sweatshirts, caps, or other markers about 5 feet apart in a straight line. (Really good dribblers can set the markers closer together, while newer dribblers can move them farther apart.) Weave in and out of the markers while dribbling. Pretend that each marker is a defensive player. Keep switching hands so that you keep your body between the ball and the defenders. Don't watch the ball—keep your head up!

On Your Back Drill

Stand still and dribble the ball with your right hand. Still dribbling, get down on your knees. Dribble on your knees for a minute, then keep dribbling as you sit down. Dribble while sitting for a minute, then keep dribbling while you lie down (Figure 2-11). Now dribble the ball around your head to your left hand. Now sit up and dribble, then kneel and dribble, then stand and dribble.

2-11 ON YOUR BACK: Dribbling while standing is a simple drill, but try it while lying down on the floor. This drill challenges you to go from standing to sitting to lying down without losing control of the ball. Once you've accomplished that, try it with the opposite hand.

To Dribble or Not to Dribble

How do you know *when to dribble and when not to*?

Many players start dribbling as soon as they receive a pass. They look around while they dribble the ball. Now they've already used up their dribble. And because their head is up, looking for a chance to pass or shoot, the ball isn't as safe as if it were held.

If you start dribbling right away, and the defense is right on you, you will have to stop dribbling to keep them from stealing the ball. Now that the defense knows you don't have a dribble left, they can really get in close. If you still had your dribble, the defender would have to hang back in order to see where you were going to go with it. Only dribble when you have a plan. Dribble if you need to:

- Bring the ball up the court.
- Get the ball away from a defender.
- Drive toward the basket.

If you don't have a plan, don't dribble. Don't dribble in traffic. If you are in the center of a group of defensive players, and you try to dribble, you'll be outnumbered. Try to pass the ball instead. Dribbling works best when you have only one defender guarding you. Don't dribble when you need to move the ball down the court quickly. Passing is faster.

Make It Up, Play It Out

Here are two games that you can play with your friends to help you with your ball handling skills.

Bull in the Ring

For this game you need three or more players, a basketball for each player, and a play area with a hard surface, such as a driveway or part of a basketball court.

2-12

If the play area is small, like a driveway, then the driveway is the whole play area. If you use a larger area, mark off a big circle for the play area. Inside the circle, players dribble their balls with one hand while using their free hand to try to knock the other players' balls out of the circle (Figure 2-12). Fouling other players is not allowed. When a player loses his ball, he has to leave the circle. The last player left in the circle is the winner.

2-12 BULL IN THE RING: This drill forces you to protect your ball while trying to swipe away someone else's. It's a great drill to improve peripheral vision and court awareness.

Snakes Against Lizards

For this game, you need four or more players, one basketball for every two players, and a small play area such as a driveway or part of a basketball court.

Half the players are snakes and the other half are lizards. The snakes dribble the balls, while the lizards try to knock the balls out of the play area. Fouling another player is not allowed. After losing the ball, a snake can stay in the play area and catch a pass from any other snake.

When all the basketballs have been knocked out of the area, the lizards dribble the balls. The team that knocks all the balls out of the play area in the shortest time, wins the game.

Outside the Lines

NO DRIBBLING!
When basketball was invented there was no dribbling at all! Players could only pass the ball or shoot. Players couldn't move around the court when they had the ball. They could only move one foot as long as the other one stayed planted.

Keep Focused

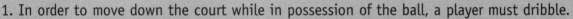

1. In order to move down the court while in possession of the ball, a player must dribble.
2. Dribbling is done with only one hand at a time.
3. Players are allowed only one non-stop stretch of dribbling for each possession of the ball.
4. When dribbling, stay low to the ground and keep your hands, arms, and legs loose.
5. Keep your body between the ball and the defensive player.
6. Keep your head up.
7. Make sure you can dribble equally well with both hands.
8. Practice your dribbling skills every day.

CHAPTER 3

Passing

Passing the ball to one of your teammates is the fastest way to move the ball up the court. That's why passing is the most important skill in basketball. Learning to pass takes a lot of practice. Not only do you need to practice the correct ways to handle the ball when passing, you also need to learn how to pass the ball to your teammates. You need to know who moves slowly and who moves quickly. You need to know how high each of your teammates can jump to catch a pass. A good passing team is one where each player knows the other players' moves.

Basic Passes

There are four basic passes: the chest pass, the bounce pass, the baseball pass, and the handoff.

The Chest Pass

The *chest pass* is used more than any other pass. It's a two-handed pass that moves the ball in a straight line from one player to another. It's the fastest pass you can use.

Grip the ball with both hands, one on each side of the ball. Your fingers should be spread wide apart with your thumbs almost touching each other on the back of the ball. Bend your elbows and bring the ball close to your chest. Take a step toward your teammate as you push your arms out in front of you and release the ball. Throw the ball straight at your teammate's chest (Figure 3-1).

Put some muscle behind your pass. You don't want to knock your teammate off his feet with a too-powerful pass, but you want the ball to go straight and fast.

Use the chest pass for mid-range passes. You will be using other types of passes for long or short distances. Use the chest pass to move the ball quickly around the key (free-throw lane), or to move the ball up the court when you're trying to break a press (when the defenders are tightly guarding you).

3-1 CHEST PASS: Bring the ball into the chest with both hands, head up and eyes set on the receiver. Step toward the target and give a crisp pass chest level. The hands should be pointed down and out in the follow through.

Outside the Lines

THE CHEST PASS HAS A LOT OF ZIP
Pete Carril, retired Princeton Coach whose team upset the NCAA champions in a 1996 tournament win, believes that the chest pass is the most accurate way to pass the ball. Says Carril, "A player can throw a variety of chest passes — left, right, up, down, short, long, and the ball always starts from the same place. It leaves the hands quickly, it does not take long to release, it leaves with a lot of zip, and it is hard to intercept since its direction and velocity [speed] can be disguised."

The Bounce Pass

The *bounce pass* is a two-handed pass where the ball is bounced from one player to another. Grip the ball with both hands, one on each side of the ball. Your fingers should be spread wide apart with your thumbs almost touching each other on the back of the ball (this is the same grip that's used for the chest pass). Bend your elbows and bring the ball close to your chest. Take a step toward your teammate and throw the ball at the floor so it will bounce once and come up to your teammate's hands. Try to bounce the ball about two-thirds of the way between you and your teammate (Figures 3-2 and 3-3).

The bounce pass is not as fast as the chest pass, so put some power in it (throw it at the floor with some force) so that it will bounce high enough to get to your teammate's hands.

The bounce pass is a short pass. Use it when you have a defensive player on top of you, waving his arms around. The bounce pass allows you to pass the ball down toward the floor, away from the defender's arms.

3-2

3-2 and 3-3 BOUNCE PASS: The eyes should be looking down at a spot about two-thirds of the way to the receiver. Bring the ball into the chest with both hands, take a step and throw the ball at the spot on the floor with the hands pointed down and out in the follow through. This pass can be used to elude the arms of the defender.

3-3

Line Passing Drill

You need several players for this drill. Players form two lines that face each other with 10 or 12 feet between the two lines. The first player in line one makes a two-handed chest pass to the first player in line two. After passing, the player from line one runs to the end of line two. The player from line two, who received the pass, makes a two-handed chest pass to the next player in the other line, then moves to the end of the other line. Continue passing the ball until all the players have caught a pass. Repeat the drill, using a two-handed bounce pass.

The Baseball Pass

The baseball pass is a long, one-handed pass that is used when you want to cover a lot of ground. It's called the baseball pass because the basketball is thrown with the same motion that people use to throw a baseball (Figure 3-4).

Hold the basketball in one hand, next to your ear. Your elbow is out in front of you and your wrist is next to your ear, ready to propel the ball forward. The basketball is resting in the palm of your hand. Because this is hard to do with a big ball,

3-4

3-4 BASEBALL PASS: Bring the ball back behind the ear with the dominant arm, with the weight of the body on the rear leg. Step in the direction of the target with the front leg. Transfer the weight forward and throw the ball overhand. Follow through by bending the back. This pass is used when the receiver is a long distance away.

3-5 HANDOFF: The receiver runs off the back side of the player with the ball. The player simply hands off or flips the ball to the receiver as he runs by.

you can use your other hand to get the ball balanced in your palm.

Step forward with the foot opposite your throwing arm as you bring your arm forward and release the ball. Launch the ball high in the air so it will travel on an arc to your teammate's hands.

The baseball pass isn't used very often. Because this is a long pass, there are lots of opportunities for defenders to intercept (catch) the pass. Use the baseball pass when you need to get the ball to a teammate who is upcourt ahead of the defenders.

The Handoff

The *handoff* is a short pass where you hand the ball to a teammate who is near you.

One way to handoff the basketball is to hold the ball out to a teammate who takes it as he brushes past you.

When your teammate is too far from you to take the ball from your hands, give the ball a little flip in your teammate's direction (Figure 3-5). When handing off, the ball is passed from a player, who is heavily guarded and standing still, to a player who is in motion.

All passes, except the handoff, should be thrown with power. A slow, lazy pass will probably be intercepted before it reaches your teammate.

To Pass or Not to Pass?

How do you know *when to pass* and *when not to*?

Don't pass the ball into a crowd. Sometimes it's tempting to try to get the ball to your team's best player, but if the defense is all around him, chances are that the ball will be lost before it even gets there. Even if your teammate does receive the ball, there's still all those defenders who will work to stop the shot.

Don't pass the ball over the top of a crowd. There's a good chance that one of the defenders is a better jumper than you thought. Your teammates near you should be moving to get open. Look for them.

3-6 BEHIND-THE-BACK PASS: This pass is done on the move and can catch the defense by surprise. The player either bounces or throws the ball from behind his back to his teammate. It's most effective when the passer's eyes are looking straight ahead and not in the direction of his teammate.

Fancy Passes

When you watch a game, you will see all kinds of fancy passes. Once you're pretty good with the basic passes, you can try some fancy ones.

Behind the Back

Passing the ball behind your back can catch your opponent off guard. It's a short pass and it's done while you are moving. As you move forward, take the ball behind your back with one hand, and as you continue to move forward, flip the ball in the direction of your teammate (Figure 3-6). You can also make a bounce pass from behind your back.

Behind-the-Back Drill

This drill will get your hands used to the feel of the ball as it rolls off your fingers, just like it does when you throw a pass from behind your back. Stand still and pass the ball around the middle of your body (Figure 3-7). Circle your body with the ball twenty times without dropping the ball.

Two-Hand Overhead

If you're taller than your defender, raise the ball *over your head* with two hands. This keeps the ball away from the defender and allows you to look around to see which of your teammates are open. Snap your arms forward and throw the ball (Figures 3-8 and 3-9). This pass starts high and stays high. It's a good pass to use when you are trying to get the ball to a tall teammate who is underneath the basket.

Alley-Oop

The *alley-oop* pass is a long, high pass that is used when your teammate is going to *slam dunk*. Slam dunk means that the player jumps high enough to get their hand(s) above the basket, then slams the ball down into the basket. Throw the ball to the level of the basket. Your teammate will jump to catch the ball at the level of the basket and make the slam dunk (Figures 3-10 and 3-11).

3-7 BEHIND-THE-BACK DRILL: Start with the ball in front of you. Then pass the ball behind your back to yourself time and time again, switching hands as the ball travels around from front to back.

3-8 and 3-9 OVERHEAD PASS: Your head should be up and facing the target. Bring the ball directly behind the head with both hands, throwing the ball over top of the defender. The hands should point outward in the follow through.

3-10 and 3-11 ALLEY OOP: Give a lead pass in the vicinity of the rim. Your teammate should time his jump so that he catches the ball on his way up to the basket. Once he catches the ball, the only step remaining is to put the ball in the hoop.

Faking

Sometimes it's hard for you to get away from your defender in order to make a good pass, and other times it's hard for your teammates to shake their defenders in order to receive the pass. And there are times when a player seems open, but as soon as the pass leaves your hand, an opponent is magically sailing through the air to intercept it. What can you do to prevent this? You can *fake*.

Faking means using your body to fool the defender into thinking that you will be doing one thing, when you will really be doing something else.

Faking with Your Eyes

Don't look right at the teammate you're going to pass to. If you do, the defenders will know where the ball is going before you even throw it, and if the defenders are quick, they can intercept the pass. To make a good eye fake, find your open teammate, look away from him, and pass.

Faking with Your Head

You can use your head to make the defender think you are going to take a shot, when you're really going to pass. When taking a

3-12 and 3-13 FAKE AND PASS: Step toward a teammate and pump fake the ball as if it were going to be a pass to him. Step back with the front foot and pivot in the direction of another teammate, giving him a crisp chest pass. The defender will be out of position, giving a clear lane to make an accurate pass.

INBOUND PASS RULE
Players have five seconds to pass the ball inbounds to a teammate after taking possession of the ball.

shot, a player's head naturally tilts upward so they can see the basket. Right before you make your pass, tilt your head back to make the defender think you are going to shoot. The defender will get ready to block high to stop your shot and you can throw a low bounce pass.

Faking with Your Arms

Thrust your arms out with the ball in the direction of a teammate on your right. Your defender should lunge that way to try to stop the pass. At that moment, snatch your arms back and send the pass off toward a teammate on your left (Figures 3-12 and 3-13). You need to be very quick throwing the real pass because the defender won't be fooled for long.

To make a good fake, you have to be a convincing actor. A weak movement in the wrong direction isn't going to fool anyone.

Special Passes

There are some special passes that are used only at certain times during a game.

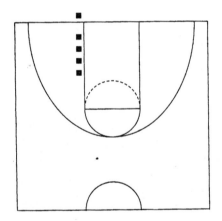

Inbound Pass

After a basket has been made, or after certain fouls, the ball is taken out of bounds and must be *passed back into bounds* in order to start the play. The opponents will be guarding against the inbound pass very tightly, so it's important for the players who might be receiving the pass to keep moving around to get away from the defenders. The inbounder will then pass to any player who is open.

If the inbound pass is after a basket, the passer is allowed to run back and forth behind the end line, to help confuse the defenders.

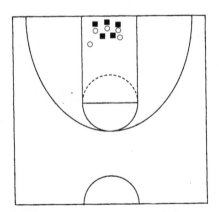

The Outlet Pass

The *outlet pass* is used after a *defensive rebound*. A rebound is when a shot hits the rim or backboard, misses the basket and rebounds back toward the floor. A defensive rebound means that the missed shot was caught by a defensive player.

As soon as you see that your teammate has rebounded the ball, break (run) to the sideline as fast as you can. Then, as soon as your teammate has the ball under control, he can pivot toward you and pass you the ball. This gets the ball up the court quickly and away from the crowd under the basket.

Receiving the Pass

When you *receive* (catch) a pass, use both hands. Get your thumbs behind the ball the same way you would if you were throwing a chest pass. Try to make the catch with your fingers and elbows bent. Stand up on the balls of your feet when the pass is coming because you may have to move your body to get behind the ball. If the ball goes through your hands, your body will stop it.

Getting Open

Before you can receive a pass, you have to get open (away from the defenders). Here's how:

1. **Move quickly and aggressively.** A player who slowly jogs around the court is never going to get free. You must sprint and make sharp turns.

2. **Know where you are going.** Know where the ball is and where your teammates are. If everyone is running toward the ball, then you run away from it to avoid the crowd.

3. **Get out of the way if you're not helping.** If you make a cut toward the ball and can't get in the clear, then move away from the ball, causing your defender to come with you. Then try your move again.

4. **Pay attention to the person guarding you.** If your defender is moving in one direction, than you go the other way. If your defender isn't paying close attention to you, cut toward the basket.

5. **Stay close to your defender until you make your move.** If you're close to the defender and you make a sharp cut toward or away from the ball, you'll be one step ahead of him. If you're far away from the defender when you make your cut, then he will have time to stop you.

6. **Fake and break.** Fake like you're going to cut one way, then cut the other way.

Converse® All Star™ Profile
Denny Crum

Q **A** *What are the traits you look for in a player?*

You have to work hard and dedicate yourself to improving. You'd be amazed at how many kids who, if they worked harder, would become more successful.

Q **A** *What are the basketball skills and physical attributes you look for?*

I look for quickness. You can do so many things with quickness. Especially with the importance of the three-point shot, I look for good shooting ability.

Q **A** *How many plays do you teach your offense?*

By the end of the year, we might have 15 plays. We try to add a little bit each week, trying to incorporate things that have options. A lot of our plays depend on what the defense takes away.

Q **A** *What can players learn from competing in the game of basketball that will help them in life?*

Playing basketball helps you learn to get along with people, learn to give to the betterment of the team. Basketball also helps you develop good work habits and the ability to organize and manage your time.

Q **A** *What gives you the most satisfaction as a coach?*

I enjoy the responsibility of being an important influence in players' lives. It's satisfying when you watch them become a success in life, whether it's as a lawyer or recreation director or whatever the player chooses.

Q **A** *What is the most difficult part of your job?*

Recruiting is very difficult. And getting people to accept their role, whether it's as a practice player or defensive specialist. Trying to get players to put the team first—ahead of personal goals—is a very challenging part of the job.

V Sprint Drill

This drill is done without the ball. It will give you practice making the kind of sharp cuts that you need in order to get clear of a defender to catch a pass. Start at one end of the court. Sprint to the other end as fast as you can, but as you sprint, change direction ten times before you reach the other end. Make each direction change a sharp, quick, cut. As you make your cuts, you will be running down the court in a zigzag pattern, making V's. You want to make narrow V's, not wide ones.

Make It Up, Play It Out

Here's two games that will help you develop good passing skills.

Target

For this game you need two players, a basketball, a play area with a hard surface, and a *target* (something like a stick or a coin).

Players stand several feet apart and place the target between them. Players bounce pass the ball back and forth to each other, aiming the bounce at the target. Each time a player hits the target, he gets one point. The first player to get ten points and be at least two points ahead of the other player, wins the game.

Monkey in the Middle

You need three players, a basketball, and a play area with a hard surface. To start the game, the three players line up several feet apart. The two players on the ends, pass the ball back and forth, and the player in the middle tries to steal the ball without fouling. The two players on the ends are allowed to dribble the ball between passes. When the middle player manages to steal the ball, he trades places with the player who lost the ball. Now that person becomes the *monkey in the middle*.

Keep Focused

1. It takes teamwork to make a good pass.
2. Put some power into your passes.
3. Don't pass the ball into an area that's crowded with defenders.
4. The chest pass, the bounce pass, the baseball pass, and the handoff are the four basic passes.
5. Use your eyes, head, and arms to fake the defensive players.
8. Move to get open.

CHAPTER 4

Shooting

Imagine that your team is ahead by four points. There are two minutes left in the game and you have to protect your lead. In order to keep the ball away from the other team, your teammates are passing the ball around the key. The ball is passed to you. Your defender is all over you, slapping at the ball. He fouls you. Tweet! The referee blows the whistle. Because of the foul, you get a free throw (shot from the free throw line without interference from the other team). You've practiced this shot a million times. You could almost do it in your sleep. You line the shot up, the gym gets quiet. You take aim and *swish*—the ball goes through the basket!

The Basics of Good Shooting

If you want to hear the *swish,* then you've got to practice shooting—over, and over, and over, and over. It takes practice to make a great shooter, but before you practice, you need to know the basics of good shooting.

Spin

Spin means that the ball turns, or spins, while it's in the air. The direction in which the balls spins depends on how you release the ball as you throw it. If your body is crooked when you throw, or if you throw with both hands, you put a sideways spin on the ball. This *bad spin* will keep the ball from going where you aimed it. When you shoot for the basket, the only *good spin* is a backspin. When a ball is spinning backward and it hits the rim of the basket or the backboard, the ball tends to drop into the basket instead of bouncing off the rim or backboard in another direction. To get good spin on the ball, use the four basic steps for good shooting: square up to the basket, use your strong hand to shoot, create a shooting window, and follow through.

4-1 PLAYER BEFORE SHOT: Square your feet and shoulders to the basket. Bend your knees and keep the elbows in. Lock your eyes on the hoop.

Squaring Up

When you take a shot, you should face the basket with both of your shoulders the same distance from the basket. This is called *squaring up* (Figure 4-1). If you shoot while your body isn't square to the basket, you will put bad spin on the ball and it won't go where you aim it.

Your Hands

Shoot the ball with your *dominant hand* (right for righties, left for lefties). This is your *strong hand*, and it should be centered and spread wide on the ball (Figure 4-2). To find the center of the ball, place the middle finger of your shooting hand over the small hole that's used to pump air into the ball. Spread the rest of your fingers out wide.

Use your other hand, or *weak hand*, to guide the ball. Place your weak hand on the side of the ball to give you more control. Use your weak hand to help you support the ball, but not to shoot the ball. If you use both hands to shoot the ball, you will put bad spin on the ball.

4-2 HAND CENTERED: Place your shooting hand in the middle of the ball. Spread your fingers as far apart as possible to cover as much area on the ball as you can; this will give you good control. Place your non-shooting hand on the side for additional control and support.

The Shooting Window

If you bring the ball up in front of your face, then you won't be able to see the basket. If you bring the ball over one shoulder, you'll be able to see the basket, but you will put bad spin on the ball. Bring the ball up to your forehead, so your arms will create a *window* for you to look through as you take your shot. Keep your elbows in close to your body and keep your hands near the sides of your head. Look through the window at the basket.

When you start your shot at the level of your forehead, your arms won't have as much power as they would at chest height. To make up for that you can use power from your legs by bending your knees and then straightening them as you shoot. Another way to take power from your legs is to jump as you shoot the ball.

As you take your shot, your legs bend, your arms spring forward, and your wrist snaps. The basketball should roll off your three middle fingers. This will put a slight backspin on the ball, which is the only spin that you want. If you've done everything right, the ball will sail in a beautiful, high arc toward the basket. The closer you are to the basket, the higher you should make the arc of your shot.

4-3 FOLLOW THROUGH: After the ball is released, fully extend your shooting arm. Keep your eyes locked on the target.

Follow Through

After you've released the ball you have to follow through. This means that you continue your throwing motion by fully extending your throwing arm and letting your wrist drop forward (Figure 4-3). When you finish the follow through, your arm should look like the neck and head of a goose—your arm is up in the air with the elbow straight, and your fingers are pointing down to the ground. Leave your arm up in the air until the ball goes through the basket.

If you have trouble remembering to follow through, try saying a reminder word each time you shoot. The word can be "snap," or "goose," or "through."

Around the World Shooting Drill

Pick out seven spots that are spaced in an arc around the outside of the free throw lane. The first spot should be near one side of the basket. Shoot from the first spot until you make a basket. Then move on to the next spot. Keep shooting until you've made a basket from all seven spots. Then start the drill over, shooting from the last spot, first.

Kinds of Shots

Once you've practiced the basics, you're ready to learn how to make shots in a game. Unless you're taking a free throw, the other team is not going to let you just stand there and set up for a perfect shot. You have to shoot off a dribble, or immediately after receiving a pass. You need to square up as fast as possible, but don't rush the shot—make it the same slow, even shot that you've practiced. Here's some different kinds of shots:

Jump Shot

The *jump shot* is done off a dribble. Pick the ball up from the dribble, square up to the basket, and jump as you shoot. After shooting, you should land on the same spot that you jumped from, or slightly ahead of your take-off point.

The Lay-up

The *lay-up* is a one-handed shot from one side of the basket. It is the easiest shot to make because you are shooting very close to the basket. When shooting the lay-up, it's very important to look up at the basket. If you don't, you might be too close to the basket when you shoot, and you'll miss. When you're coming toward the basket for the lay-up, dribble with your head up and look at the basket while you get into position.

If you go in for the lay-up on the right side of the basket, you will jump off your left foot and shoot with your right hand. If you go in on the left side of the basket, you will jump off your right foot and shoot with your left hand. You should be able to shoot a lay-up with either hand.

As you near the basket, plan your steps so that your inside foot (the one closest to the basket) will take the last step before you go up in the air. When you plant the inside foot, make sure it is turned toward the basket so that you can square up your body as you jump. As soon as you plant your inside foot, raise your outside leg and your outside arm (which has the ball) up toward the hoop, and jump up off the planted foot. You will be shooting from the side of the basket, so when you release the ball, aim for the backboard so that the ball will bounce off the backboard and into the basket (Figure 4-4). If you use the basic steps of good shooting, as described above, the ball will have the correct spin and go in the basket.

The Power Lay-up

The *power lay-up*, is a lay-up from a standing position under the basket. You jump with both hands on the ball to protect it. Use the power lay-up when you receive the ball under that basket. The power lay-up will help you push the ball up through the defenders' arms so you have a clear shot at the basket. The power lay-up is mostly used by taller players who can jump higher than the defenders.

Before shooting the ball, square up, then throw your whole body into the jump to make sure you get above the defenders. Hold onto the ball tightly until you release it.

4-4 LAY-UP: Make the foot closer to the basket your takeoff foot (last step as you go to the air off the dribble). Lay the ball off the backboard, with your arm nearer to the basket. Keep your eyes focused on the basket throughout.

The Reverse Lay-up

The *reverse lay-up* begins on one side of the basket and ends on the other. Use this shot when the defender is very close and can block a regular lay-up. Close in on one side of the basket, but instead of planting your foot and going up for a shot, dribble under the basket to the other side. This will help you get away from the defender. Now that you are on the other side of the basket, shoot the ball on the same side of your body that you would have used if

4-5 to 4-7 REVERSE LAY-UP (Starting from the left-hand side): Approach the basket as if you were going to execute a normal lay-up from the left side. Take an extra dribble to position yourself for take-off a little closer to the basket. Leap into the air off the inside foot but hold onto the ball until you're under the opposite side of the basket and lay the ball off the backboard with the right hand.

you had done the lay-up on the other side of the basket (Figures 4-5 to 4-7). (If your drive began toward the left side of the basket, you will shoot from the right of the basket, but you will do a left-handed lay-up.)

Bank Shot

In the *bank shot,* the ball is banked (bounced) off the backboard before it goes into the basket. The bank shot can be risky because you are bouncing it off the backboard instead of shooting straight into the basket.

You need to be about 10 feet from the basket and off to one side to try a bank shot. Never try a bank shot from straight down the middle. Before shooting, square up to the basket. Shoot the ball so that it hits the top corner of the box (square drawn on the backboard) on the side that you are shooting from. Your shot should have a slow, easy arc and hit the corner of the box as it's coming down.

Hook Shot

The *hook shot* is a one-handed shot, thrown when you're close to the basket. You shoot the ball over the top of your head with one hand, so the ball hooks (curves) toward the basket in an arc (Figure 4-8). On the hook shot, you don't square up to the basket before shooting. The hook shot begins with your back to the basket and the ball in both hands. If you are going to shoot the hook with your right hand, turn to the left by pivoting on your left foot so your body is at a right angle to the basket. Look up at the basket and switch the ball to

4-8 HOOK SHOT: Turn your body away from the defender to protect the ball. Reach high into the air and toss the ball into the basket with a sweeping arm motion. Let the ball roll off your fingertips.

your right hand. Bring your right arm straight out to your side, then swing your hand straight up above your head in a wide arc and release the ball at the top of the arc. Let the ball roll off your fingertips.

Slam Dunk

When a player jumps up above the rim and slams the ball down into the basket it's called a *slam dunk* (Figure 4-9). You don't have to be a giant or have feet made of springs in order to slam dunk, but you must be tall enough and be able to jump high enough to get above the rim. Most coaches think that a player should be six feet tall to be able to slam dunk.

To practice for the slam dunk, start by doing lay-ups. When you go up, just lay the ball over the rim so it tips into the basket. Keep practicing until you get to the point where your knuckles can touch the rim. Your next goal is to get enough height so that the back of your hand touches the rim as you lay the ball over the edge. Once that happens, you're ready to slam dunk. After slam dunking, you can grab the rim if you need to in order to come back down safely.

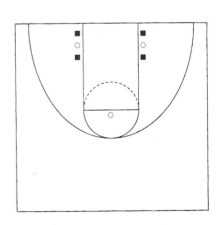

4-9 SLAM DUNK: This is a shot for tall players or great leapers. Go up for the shot as if it were a normal lay-up. Raise your entire hand over the rim and slam the ball down through the basket. It's not necessary to palm the ball when you dunk.

Combination Shooting Drill

Stand about three feet away from the basket, and without dribbling, shoot the ball one-handed. When you can make five shots in a row, start with your back to the basket. Pivot (swing around on one foot) to face the basket, then shoot. Keep pivoting and shooting until you can make five shots in a row. Now add dribbling. Pivot, dribble, then shoot. It helps if you have a friend throw the ball to you before every shot. Then you can practice catching the ball, pivoting, dribbling, and shooting in quick order.

Free Throw

After you are fouled by a defender, you get one or more *free throws*. For a free throw, you stand on the free throw line and face the basket. Your teammates and the defensive players line up around the free throw lane. Because the defenders are not allowed to interfere, you can really concentrate on your shot. A good high school player should make about seventy percent of his free throws. Here are some tips that can help you be accurate on your free throws (Figure 4-10):

1. **Make sure the foot on the same side as your shooting hand is slightly out in front.** This will help you release the ball from the center of your body.

2. **Keep it simple.** Don't distract yourself by a lot of showy ball bouncing.

4-10

4-10 FREE THROW: Square your feet and shoulders with the basket. The foot on your shooting side should be slightly in front of the other to ensure that the ball will be released in the center of the body. Focus on the front of the rim. Take a deep breath and shoot the ball the exact same way every time. Make sure your practice a good follow through.

3. **Shoot the exact same shot every time.** Free throws can be thrown underhand or overhead (from above your head). Decide how you will make your free throw shots and do it the same way every time. The free throw should be practiced by itself, so you know exactly how to shoot, every time you step up to the foul line.

4. **Take your time.** It's an important shot, so make sure you catch your breath before shooting. Your teammates will probably appreciate the breather, too.

Free throws can be very important in winning games. About twenty-five percent of all games are won by the success of free throws.

Practice, Practice, Practice

Like any sport, basketball takes lots of practice. Repeating the motions used in shooting is the only way to train your body to know how to move and how much force is needed for each kind of shot. When it comes to practice, young players are usually driveway shooters or pickup players. You want to be both.

Driveway Shooters

Driveway shooters are kids who spend hours out in their driveway, taking shots from different angles and different distances until their accuracy is pretty good—until game time. Then their beautiful shots fall apart because they're running, they're tired, and the defenders are all over them. They almost never get a perfect, open shot like they do in the driveway.

The *pickup player* goes to the playground every time he wants to play, and he joins in a game. He's in shape, he knows what it's like to shoot with distractions, and he knows how to get the defense out of his face. But during a game, his shots don't go in. That's because he hasn't practiced taking those perfect shots like the driveway shooter has. So you want to practice both ways: alone in the driveway, and with other players.

Count Your Shots

To be a good shooter, you have to shoot between 300 and 500 regular shots a day and about 100 free throws. It sounds like a lot, but it only takes a couple of hours. Having a friend pass you the ball before you shoot is a good idea. Make sure at least a third of your shots are off a dribble.

Keep track of your progress. Count how many shots you make from each spot on the court, then write down the number. After several practice sessions, you can see how much you've improved.

Game Time

Here are a few things to keep in mind when shooting in a game:

The Three-Point Line

During a game, always be aware of the *three-point line* (the large half-circle drawn on the floor around the basket). Shots made from outside the line are worth three points. Shots made from inside the line are worth two points. Don't shoot the ball if you're only one foot inside the line. Take a step backward and go for the extra point.

Shoot What You Know

When you're playing in a game, use only those shots that you've been practicing. If you never practice shooting from the three-point line, the game is not the place to try it. Without practice, chances are good that you'll miss. Your team will be better off if you try to work the ball inside the three-point line for a shot that you've been practicing. The trick here is to make sure you practice all the shots you'll need in a game.

Outside the Lines

UNDERHAND VERSUS OVERHEAD FREE THROWS
A City of New York University physicist named Peter J. Brancazio studied underhand and overhead free throw shots. He found that the underhand is better because it naturally puts more backspin on the ball. Still, most of today's players use the overhead shot. Rick Barry was the last of the great underhand free throw shooters. Since 1980, he has held the NBA record for the highest career free throw percentage (.900), and he did it with overhead shots.

These games will make shooting practice fun for you and your friends.

Shoot and Rebound

To play this game, you need four or more players, two balls, and a half court. Players form two lines. One is the shooting line and one is the rebounding line. The first player in the shooting line dribbles in and shoots a lay-up, while the player from the rebounding line comes in to get the rebound. The players then go to the end of the opposite line.

If a player misses his lay-up, he goes to the rebounding line and stays there, rebounding all the time. The last player left in the shooting line is the winner. This game can also be played with jump shots instead of lay-ups.

Horse

You need two or more players and a half court. The first player takes a shot. If he misses, then the next player may take any shot he pleases. However, if the first player makes the shot, then the next player must copy that shot exactly.

If the second player makes this exact same shot, then the first player (or the third player if there is more players) must do the shot again. This goes on until someone misses. That person has an "H." The next person in line decides which shot will be tried next. Every time a player misses, they get a letter in the word "horse." A player is out of the game when he has spelled out the word, H-O-R-S-E. The last player left is the winner.

Twenty-One

You need two or more players and a half court. Draw a curved line (an arc) on the pavement. Draw the line out from the basket about where the free throw line would be.

The first player takes a shot from behind the line. If he makes it, he gets three points. If not, he rushes in to get the rebound and takes a second shot from the place where he retrieves the ball, no matter where it is. If he makes this shot, he gets two points. Finally, the player takes the ball in for a lay-up. This counts as one point. Each time the player has the ball, he has a chance to get a total of six points.

Then it's the next player's turn. Play continues until a player reaches twenty-one points. However, players must reach twenty-one exactly or they have to start over at zero. Therefore, if a player has nineteen points, he will deliberately try to miss the shot from behind the line and miss his lay-up shot.

1. Square up to the basket.
2. Center you shooting hand on the ball.
3. Create a shooting window with your arms.
4. Follow through.
5. Get power from your legs by bending them or jumping as you shoot.
6. Practice shooting alone and with other players.
7. When doing a lay-up, keep your head up, and be sure to bounce the ball off the backboard.
8. Make your free shots the same way every time.
9. If you don't practice it, don't shoot it in a game.

CHAPTER 5

Rebounding

When a shot misses and bounces off the backboard or the rim, that's a *rebound*. An *offensive rebound* is when the a player from the team that took the shot catches the ball. A *defensive rebound* is when a player from the other team catches the ball. When there's a rebound, all the players under the basket go for the ball. Being able to out jump the opponents can help you get the rebound, but you also need the four basic rebounding skills: get the inside position, box out, grab the ball, and get control.

Get the Inside Position

When you are closer to the basket than your opponent, than you have the *inside position*. When you're in the inside position, you have a much better chance of getting the rebound. There are two tricks to getting the inside position:

1. **See the ball at all times.** If you're watching the ball, you can react as soon as it's shot. Before it even gets to the basket, you can be in position for the rebound. Always think that every shot is going to miss, so you'll be ready when one does.

2. **Get close to your opponent.** As soon as the shot has been taken, go to your opponent if he's not already right

5-1 and 5-2 BOX OUT: Once the ball is shot into the air, the defensive player should turn himself to face the basket keeping himself between the basket and his man. Push your rear end into the player and keep your feet moving so he can't move around you. Keep your eyes on the basket and use your arm to keep a feel for where the offensive player is.

on top of you. If you're touching him, you have a better chance of keeping track of him while you are watching the ball. It will also be easier for you to get past him to get the inside position.

Box Out

Once you've got the inside position, you have to keep it. Do this by turning your butt toward the opponent's stomach and moving backward. This move is called *boxing out* (Figures 5-1 and 5-2).

Keep the opponent behind your body, so that he will have to leap over you in order to rebound the ball. If he tries, he will probably foul you.

Make sure you keep moving while you box out. If you just stand still, your opponent can sneak around behind you. Keep your feet wide apart and your body low while you box out. Keep the opponent on your back until the last possible second before jumping for the rebound. If you jump up to get the ball too soon, then the opponent might be able to get around you.

Size doesn't mean a whole lot in boxing out. Even if your opponent is taller than you, if you can keep him on your back, his ability to jump higher won't do him much good. It's kind of like a small, yappy dog getting in the way of a horse—it can work.

Box Out Drill

Players pair up around the court and jog around together. Both players in a pair try to gain the inside position, yet they're not allowed to touch each other until the coach calls, "shot." At that moment, everyone boxes out.

Grab the Ball

After you've grabbed the inside position and boxed out your opponent, go after the rebound. If other players around you are jumping for the ball, then jump off with both feet to get the most power you can (Figure 5-3). If you're in the clear, you can jump faster and higher by jumping off one foot.

Always use two hands to get the ball, because there will be lots of defenders right there to take it away from you. If you can't grab the ball with both hands, tip it toward your teammate.

Get Control

Once you have the ball, protect like it was worth a million dollars. Bring it down with both arms to chest level. Use your body as a shield and pivot away from your opponent. Keep your head up so you can see what's going on, and put your elbows out to help protect the ball. Be careful not to swing your elbows or you might foul another player. Don't dribble the ball under the basket with all those defenders right there. They'll steal it for sure.

Outside the Lines

A GREAT REBOUNDER

Wilt Chamberlain was a great all-around basketball player. He once scored 100 points in a single game! But Chamberlain made his biggest contribution to his teams by rebounding. He still holds the record in every single NBA rebounding category:

**Most rebounds in a career
23,924**

**Most rebounds in a season
2,149**

**Most rebounds in a game
55**

5-3 PLAYER UP FOR A REBOUND: Try to use both feet when leaping off the floor for a rebound. The arms should extend out for the ball as the body goes up. Grab the ball with both hands so it's secure on the way down.

Offensive Rebounding

When your team has the ball, then your team is the offense. When your teammate shoots, never think that the ball will go in the basket. Think that the shot is going to miss and get into position to jump for it. Most shots from one side of the basket will rebound off the other side of the basket. Go after the rebound as hard as you can without fouling.

If you get the rebound, put the ball right back up to the basket. Don't hesitate or someone will be in your face. The only time that you might not want to put it right back up would be if your team is ahead and you are trying to take some time off the clock. If that's the case, then just get the ball back out in the front court.

Offensive Rebound Shooting Drill

This is a drill that you can do alone. Throw the ball against the backboard, grab the rebound, and immediately put it back up for a shot. If it misses, get the rebound again, and shoot until you make it. Then throw it off the backboard and start all over.

Defensive Rebounding

When the other team has the ball, then your team is the defense. Defensive players are usually in a better position for rebounds because they already have the inside position. (If the other team has the ball, then the defenders will already be under the basket before the offensive player shoots.)

When your team is on defense, there are two ways to guard the other team: zone or player-to-player. In *zone* defense, each defender guards a certain area of the court. In *player-to-player* defense, each defender guards a certain offensive player.

If you're guarding player-to-player, box out your opponent. If you're guarding a zone, quit your zone and find an opponent to box out.

If you get the rebound, look for one of your teammates who might be open for an outlet pass. If there's no one open, then bring the ball down to your chest and hold it until the traffic clears (Figure 5-4). Then you can calmly dribble it up the court or pass it off to a teammate.

Line Bounding Drill

Players line up, one behind another. The first player tosses the ball at the backboard (you don't want to make a basket). The next person in line jumps up to get the ball, then throws it against the backboard. The next person gets that rebound and throws the ball against the backboard for the next person, and so on. After taking their turn, players go to the end of the line.

5-4 AFTER REBOUND: Bring the ball into the body and lean forward to protect the ball. The player can then pass to a teammate, pivot to look up-floor for an open teammate, or dribble the ball himself.

Outside the Lines

HOW MANY MILES IN A GAME?
Ben Peck, coach at Middlebury, Vermont, once put pedometers on his players' feet to measure how far they traveled in a game. His team covered a total of 24.01 miles. Forward Fred Lapham ran the farthest, 5.31 miles. Center Bob Adsit ran 4.25 miles, and the guards averaged 2.66 miles each.

Make It Up, Play It Out

These games will improve your rebounding skills.

Mush Ball

You need two or more players, a basketball, and a half court. One player starts the game by throwing the ball against the backboard. All the players jump for the rebound. Whoever gets the rebound puts it back up for a shot. If it misses, everyone goes after the ball, but if it goes in, then the person who took the shot gets two points and goes to the foul line. The player takes free throws, getting one point for each basket, until he misses. Then Mush Ball starts all over again with the rebound. The first person to get twenty-one points is the winner.

Superbounder

You need two players, a basketball, a timer (a wristwatch will work), and a backboard or wall. One player watches the timer, and the other player is the rebounder. The rebounder stands to the right side and bounces the ball off the backboard or wall so the ball will rebound to the left. The rebounder leaps over to the left to catch the rebound, then puts the ball back up for another rebound to the right.

The rebounder does twenty rebounds from side to side while the other player times how long it takes. Then the players trade places. The player who takes the least amount of time to do twenty rebounds is the winner.

This is a fast and tiring game. If the number of rebounds are too many, then do less than twenty.

1. See the ball at all times.
2. Get close to your opponent.
3. Box out.
4. Get control of the ball.
5. Always think the shot will miss, so you're ready for the rebound.
6. Offensive rebounders should go right back up for another shot.
7. Defensive rebounders should try for an outlet pass. If no teammates are open, then hold the ball until traffic clears.

CHAPTER

Offense

During a basketball game, players shoot, rebound, dribble, and pass, over and over, at top speed. And yet every player is right where they're supposed to be, doing the right thing, at the right time for their team. How do they do it? They're using *strategy* (a plan) given to them by their coach. Your coach will decide which strategies your team will use, based on the talents of your team's players and the weaknesses of the other team's players. It's up to you and your teammates to follow the plan while playing in the game.

Each team really has two strategies: one for playing offense and one for playing defense. This chapter describes basic strategies of offense. When your team is on offense they have the ball and they are trying to score.

Playing Positions

There are five *positions* on a basketball team. Each position has a name and a number. The numbers are used on diagrams to identify the positions, and sometimes coaches refer to their players by the number of their position. (The numbers

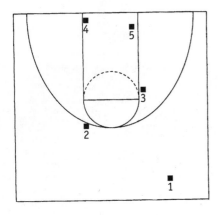

on the uniforms are *player* numbers, *not* position numbers.) Here are the numbers and the positions:

1. **Point Guard.** This player is responsible for dribbling the ball up the court, and for directing the offense.

2. **Shooting Guard.** This player stays at the top of the free throw lane and is a good shooter from outside the key.

3. **Swing Forward.** This player either stays under the basket or plays at the top of the free throw lane.

4. **Power Forward.** This player stays near the post player and is a good rebounder.

5. **Center or Post Player.** This is usually the tallest or strongest person on the team, who plays right under the basket. The post player is a top rebounder.

All five players can shoot, pass, and dribble. Scoring is a team effort, but each player is responsible for using basic offensive strategy.

Offensive Moves with the Ball

6-1 TRIPLE THREAT: In this position, you're ready to dribble, shoot or pass the ball to a teammate.

The Triple Threat

When you have the ball there are three things you can do with it: shoot, pass, or dribble. The defenders have to guard against this *triple threat*. Guarding against a shot is different than guarding against a pass or a dribble (Figure 6-1). The defender will watch you closely to guess what you are going to do with the ball.

When you receive a pass, be on the balls of your feet, catch the ball in both hands, and square up to (turn to face) the basket. Now you're in the triple threat position, meaning that you're ready to shoot, or pass, or dribble. Having these three options (choices) gives you a great advantage over the defense because they don't know which option you're going to use. Always get into the triple threat position when you get the ball, then decide what option you will use.

Your first option is to shoot. Check to see whether or not you have a good shot at the basket. If you're open and close enough to the basket to make the shot, go ahead and shoot.

If you don't have a good shot, then consider passing. See if you can get the ball off to a teammate who's in a good position to get off a shot. Get the pass off as fast as you can, so your defender won't have time to guess your option and stop you.

If you don't have an open teammate, start dribbling. You can drive toward the hoop and maybe get yourself in the open to shoot, or you can just keep moving and dribbling until a teammate can get open. Dribbling is your last choice, because once you pick up that dribble, the defender knows you will either pass or shoot, and they can move in close to stop you.

Keep Moving

In order to shoot, pass, or dribble, you have to be able to get open, and the best way to do it to keep moving so your defender will have a harder time guarding you.

Combination Drill

This is a drill for two players that uses shooting, passing, and dribbling skills. The drill starts with Player One out to one side of the basket. Player Two stands just inside the midcourt line. Player One dribbles out to where he's even with the top of the key, then passes to Player Two.

Player Two dribbles to the other end of the court for a lay-up, while Player One cuts over to the other side of the court, still even with the top of the key.

Player Two gets his own rebound and dribbles out to pass to Player One, who dribbles for a lay-up at the other end of the court.

Offensive Moves without the Ball

The Pick and Roll

A *pick* is when you stand in the way of a teammate's defender, so your teammate can get free (Figures 6-2 and 6-3). After freeing your teammate with the pick, you *roll* off the defender (move away from him) toward the basket (Figures 6-4 to 6-6).

When you set a pick, think of yourself as a wall. Make your body as wide as you can and place yourself about a foot or two from your teammate's defender. Spread your feet apart a little more than shoulder width, and get low so you won't be pushed aside easily. Get your chest in front of the defender's shoulder.

6-2 and 6-3 PICK (or SCREEN): Run down and position yourself in front of your teammate's defender. Plant your feet firmly on the ground and keep your arms up close to your trunk. Hold this position until your teammate breaks free and gets open for a pass.

6-4 to 6-6 PICK AND ROLL: Two offensive players are used in this play. The player without the ball runs toward the player with the ball and sets a *pick* (stands in a stationary position). The player with the ball then dribbles past his teammate, running his defender into him. The defensive player who is guarding the player setting the pick, then has to leave his man to pick up the man with the ball. The offensive player setting the pick then *rolls* off in the direction of the basket and takes pass lofted over top for an easy lay-up.

Once you set your pick, your teammate should drive right at you and almost rub his shoulder against yours. The defender, trying to stay with your teammate, should end up running right into you.

As your teammate comes around the pick, roll (run) toward the basket with your hand out.

Picking Away from the Ball

A second pick and roll option is *picking away from the ball* (Figures 6-7 to 6-11). Pass the ball to your teammate, then run

6-7 to 6-11 PICK AWAY FROM THE BALL: The player with the ball sends a pass over to his teammate on one side of the floor and then breaks to the other side. He sets a pick for his teammate without the ball, blocking the defender from following his man. The offensive player comes off the pick, breaks toward the ball and looks for a pass in the lane. He receives the ball with two hands and goes in for an easy lay-up.

Q *What are the traits you look for in a player?*

A The three Q's. That's the IQ (intelligence quotient), the EQ (energy quotient) and RQ (responsibility quotient). IQ shows you know what you're doing, EQ shows you have the energy to do it, and RQ shows you can do it whenever the situation calls for you.

Q *What are the playing skills you require in a player?*

A I like guys who pass the ball. You couldn't ask for better testimony than watching the Chicago Bulls play. They pass, move, pass, move. Think about it, the great passers were also the best players—Magic Johnson, Elgin Baylor, Larry Bird and Michael Jordan.

Q *How many plays do you teach your offense?*

A I don't teach plays. We have a pattern, our guys know what the other guys are doing (all the time). Throw the ball to someone time after time and he should know where you're (cutting). And you should know where to get in position for another pass.

Q *Who are your favorite players? Why?*

A I've always loved to get my teams to imitate the great players. One of my favorites was Bill Russell, because of his great desire and for doing a hundred things to help you win. I've had a special fondness for Bill Bradley for the way he played. One of my all-time favorites at Princeton was Geoff Petrie. And how can you not love Larry Bird? If you're slow and can't jump, but wind up as one of the game's top five players, what does that tell you what kind of player he is?

Q *What can players learn from competing in the game of basketball that will help them in life?*

A Responsibility and teamwork are two of life's great lessons leaned from playing basketball. If you show up on time to practice, if you pass the ball to help your team, those are things that will follow you. If you're not responsible, then you won't succeed in anything.

Q *What gives you the most satisfaction as a coach?*

A The idea of bringing people together with divergent backgrounds, getting them to achieve a goal by sacrificing and integrating their skills. And of course, I like to win—it just brings everybody together.

to the opposite side of the court and set a pick for a player over there. Once your teammate (who has the ball) sees you set the pick, he looks for the teammate coming off the pick to be open for a pass. If that teammate isn't open, then the player with the ball looks to see if you're open. You should be rolling toward the basket with your hand out.

The Fake Pick

This isn't a pick at all, but a fake, to make the defenders think that you're going to set a pick when you're not. You can fake a pick toward the ball or away from the ball. Take two or three steps toward the defender who's guarding the ball, or away from the ball, just like you would if you were going to set a pick away from the ball. Then turn the other way and roll toward the basket, looking for the ball. Your defender will be counting on you setting a pick, so when you head right down the middle of the free throw lane, you'll be open to receive the pass.

Keep Moving

While your teammate has the ball, keep moving. Get free so you can receive a pass, get in a good position to take a shot, or set a pick.

Basic Post Moves

The post player under the basket is the person the team counts on for blocking shots, rebounding, and power lay-ups. If you're the post player, keep your feet wide apart, your elbows out, and your arms up. Be ready to pivot in any direction or to go for a shot. Now here's the really tough part; you need to be able to do all this with defenders hanging over you. Here's some tricks to help you out (Figure 6-12):

- **Keep contact with the defender who is guarding you.** While you are reaching out for a pass with one arm, use your other arm to *lock* (keep contact with) your defender, so you'll know where he's going.

- **Shoot quickly once you are facing the basket.** Because the defender is so close, you have to be ready to get your shot off before he can get into position to block your shot (Figures 6-13 to 6-16).

6-12 POST PLAYER: Lean into your defender with your body and use an arm to keep contact with your defender. Stretch your other arm, signaling for a pass to that side.

6-13 to 6-16 POST TO SHOT: Call for the ball with your back to the defender, reaching out with one arm. Catch the ball with both hands. As you turn, use your elbow on that side to block the defender. If you're moving to your right side, take a small step with your right foot, plant it on the floor and then swing your body around with the left foot. As you plant your left foot and face the basket, immediately go straight up in the air for the shot. It's important not to delay the shot or the defender will have time to get back into position.

- **Use both hands to catch the ball.**
- Once you have the ball, **keep it at chest level** and turn so that the defender is on your back.
- **Fake to get clear of the defender.** The defender will probably be on your back, between you and the hoop. Here are two different fakes you can use to get a shot:

  1. If you have been locking (touching) the defender with your left elbow, look and lean (but don't actually move) to your left. The defender will think you are going to go left. As soon as the defender moves to the left, step back with your right foot and try to get your foot back farther than the defender's right foot. Now the defender is still on your back, but your leg is closer to the basket than he is. Use your right arm and elbow to force the defender away. Say low so you don't lose your balance, get your weight on your back foot, square up to the basket, and take your shot.

  2. If you're on one side of the side of the basket, your defender will probably be guarding toward the center of the key (free throw lane). Drive hard with a dribble toward the end line. As soon as the defender moves toward the end line, pull back and go up for a shot.

- **Try a hook shot.** It may throw the defender off guard if you shoot the hook instead of squaring up for a jump shot (Figures 6-17 to 6-19).

6-17 to 6-19 POST TO HOOK: This shot is almost impossible to defend when done correctly. Lean against your defender, catch the pass with both hands, take a step and pivot toward the basket. Instead of squaring up for a shot, turn your body to protect the ball and extend the outside arm out for a hook shot.

Basic Teamwork

Staying Wide

It's important to keep your offense *wide* (spread out over the court). Spreading out your players means that the defenders will have to spread out in order to guard them. If one of your teammates is going to make a move, such as a fake and a drive to the basket, the less people clogging the free throw lane, the better.

Use All Your Team's Players

When you team is on offense, everyone should be moving around. That makes it harder for the defenders to guard everyone.

One way to keep your players moving is to pass the ball around as soon as it's in your team's possession. It's important to keep all the offensive players involved with the ball. If one player is not getting the ball much, the defense gets a break because they don't have to cover that player as much. By making sure all the offensive players get the ball, the defense won't know what to expect and they are kept off balance.

Two-On-One Drill

This is a drill for two offensive players and one defender. Players One and Two pass the ball back and forth as they drive up the court toward the basket. As they approach the defender, who is positioned near the foul line, they decide what moves to make, depending on how the defender moves. If the defender guards the player with the ball, than that player must pass to his partner. If the defender drops back to guard against a pass, the player with the ball must go for a lay-up. This drill teaches you that it's important to pass the ball when you are covered.

Outside the Lines

GREAT POINT GUARDS
Position number one—the point guard, is also known as the lead guard. Some of the best NBA point guards are: John Stockton of the Utah Jazz, Kevin Johnson of the Phoenix Suns, Gary Payton of the Seattle Super-Sonics, Tim Hardaway of the Miami Heat, Mark Price of the Washington Bullets, and Kenny Anderson of the Charlotte Hornets. A good point is usually the team's best passer and dribbler.

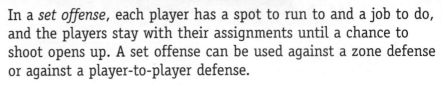

Set Offense

In a *set offense*, each player has a spot to run to and a job to do, and the players stay with their assignments until a chance to shoot opens up. A set offense can be used against a zone defense or against a player-to-player defense.

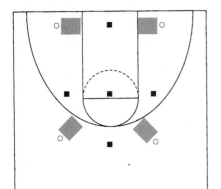

Against a Zone Defense

In the *zone defense*, each defender is assigned an area of the court to guard. When you are playing against a zone defense, the trick is to find the unguarded zones and send your players there. That way, the defenders will need to move out of their assigned zones in order to guard your team's players, and they might leave an opening.

Fake passes are also good against a zone defense, because the defenders will move to where they think the ball is going instead of staying with your player.

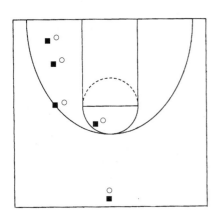

Against a Player-to-Player Defense

In the *player-to-player defense*, each defender is assigned to guard a certain offensive player. Set offenses against a player-to-player defense try to move the defenders into *unbalanced positions*, such as getting all the defenders on one side of the court or up at the top of the key. Then you can use the pick and roll to move your players into the open areas.

Set Offense Formations

The formations (arrangements of the players on the court) are called by numbers such as the one-two-two, the one-four, or the one-three-three.

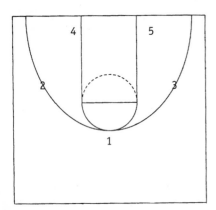

- **One-Two-Two Formation.** In this formation, player one (the point guard) is outside the three-point line in front of the basket. Players two and three are near the sidelines, one on either side of the basket. Players four and five are near the end line, one on either side of the basket. This formation leaves the center of the key open so any player can cut in the key to receive a pass. This formation is also called the give-and-go because one player passes the ball to the point guard, then cuts inside the key toward the basket. The point guard passes the ball back to that same player, who is now in position for a shot.

- **One-Four Formation.** In this formation, player one (the point guard) is outside the three-point line in front of the basket. Players two and three are outside the three-point line and near the sideline on either side of the basket. Players four and five are inside the three-point line, just outside the key. Players four and five are in a line with players two and three. This formation requires a very skilled point guard.

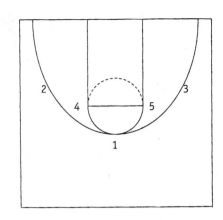

- **One-Three-One Formation.** In this formation, the point guard is outside the three-point line in front of the basket. Players two, three, and four are in a straight line across the court with players two and three out by the two sidelines, and player four centered between them in the top of the key. Player five is near the basket, to one side of the key.

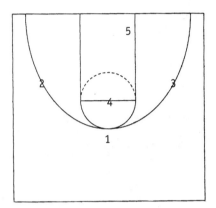

The point guard calls out the formation to the rest of the team. Most teams use code names for their formations so that the other team won't know which formation they are using. Colors can be used instead of numbers.

Freestyle Offense

In the *freestyle offense*, there is no set offense. Players are freely moving in and out of the key, around the court, or filling holes, setting picks, and trying to get open. The freestyle offense works best with fast, experienced players who know where to move to take advantage of the other team's strategy. The freestyle offense often starts with a fast break.

The Fast Break

On a *fast break*, your team passes the ball up the court very quickly after a rebound or a steal. The fast break puts immediate pressure on the defenders, and tries to get more offensive players than defensive players near the basket, so one of your players can get a quick, clear shot.

Make It Up, Play It Out

Here's a game that gives you lots of opportunities to practice your offensive strategies.

Transition Ball

For this game you need two teams of five players, a basketball, and a full court.

The game is played just like regular basketball except that two players on each team have to stay at one end of the court and two players have to stay at the other end of the court. One player from each team (the transition players) can move between the two keys. It's a three-on-three game at each end of the court. If players move out of their zone, then their team loses the ball.

Outside the Lines

WATCH THOSE BODY PARTS!

No part of an offensive player can be in the free throw lane for more than three seconds at a time. If an offensive player has even part of one foot in the lane for more than three seconds, referees can call a three-second violation and turn the ball over to the defenders. There are no time limits on how long defensive players can be in the lane.

Keep Focused

1. The triple threat is every player's basic offensive strategy.
2. Keep moving—no player should ever be caught standing still.
3. Get everyone on your team involved in the offense.
4. Keep your players spread wide.
5. Make your picks tight.
6. Don't forget to roll.
7. Use the fake.
8. Against zone defenses, find the holes.
9. Against player-to-player defenses, unbalance the players and move into the open spaces.
10. Only use a freestyle offense with experienced players.

CHAPTER 7

Defense

When the other team has the ball, then your team is playing defense. The whole point of playing defense is to keep the other team from scoring, and to get the ball back for your team. Good defense is more than just a stolen ball, a blocked shot, or a great rebound. It's teamwork that makes use of each player's defensive skills. Good defense can help your team win by stopping the other team from scoring. Even if your team scores 100 points, you still won't win if the other team scores 101.

The Defensive Stance

The defensive stance will help you move fast and stay in a good position to block a shot or steal the ball (Figure 7-1).

1. **Keep your feet a shoulder's width apart** with one foot a little in front of the other one.

2. **Keep your weight on the balls of your feet.**

3. **Keep your knees bent.**

4. **Keep your hands low and out to the sides** with your palms facing out and your fingers spread wide. From this position it will be easy to bring your arms up to block a shot, or out in front of you to stop a pass.

5. **Keep moving.** Even though you can practice this stance while standing still, when you're playing in a game, you will keep moving, either with your opponent, or within your zone.

The defensive stance may seem a bit awkward at first, but you will get used to it with practice.

7-1 DEFENSIVE STANCE: Bend slightly at the knees and waist with feet shoulder-width apart. Keep your hands out away from your body with your eyes locked on your opponent's waist. Always have the weight on the balls of your feet and keep them moving.

The Defense Shuffle Drill

This drill will increase your ability to move in the defensive stance. It will also strengthen your leg muscles. Find a place where you can see a clock with a second hand. Get into the defensive stance. Your knees should be bent, your arms out, and your head up, looking at the clock. Now get on the balls of your feet and start stepping up and down without moving forward. After five seconds of stepping in place, shuffle (slide) three steps to the left. Step in place for five more seconds, then shuffle three steps to the right. Step in place for five more seconds. Repeat. Work until you are tired. Always stop exercising if you feel pain.

Types of Defense

There are three different styles of defense: player-to-player, zone, and the combination defense.

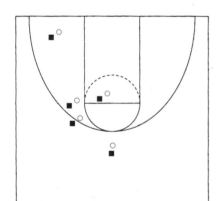

Player-to-Player Defense

In the *player-to-player defense*, each defender guards a certain offensive player. That opponent is your responsibility the minute your team is on defense.

Stay with your opponent. Use the defensive stance and stay low so you don't lose your balance if your opponent makes a quick cut (move) in another direction. Keep your eye on the ball at all times, but don't lose track of your opponent.

Player-to-player is a good defense if your players are faster than the other team's players. You'll have no trouble keeping up with your opponent.

Player-to-player is also a good defense if the other team is good at outside shots. With player-to-player defense, you can stay with your opponent when he's away from the basket and block his outside shot.

Zone Defense

In the *zone defense*, each defender is assigned to guard a certain area of the court. Stay in your zone, and stay on the move, ready to guard any opponent who comes into your zone. When an opponent enters your zone, guard him as you would in player-to-player defense until he leaves your zone. Use the defensive stance, but keep your arms high instead of out to your sides. That way, you'll be ready to stop a pass.

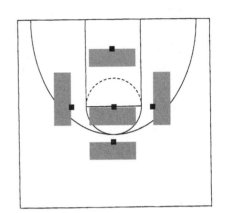

Even though you are responsible for defending your zone, there are times when you should leave it. Leave your zone to grab a loose ball, grab a rebound, or stop a shot.

The zones will cover your team's backcourt, especially the key and the areas just outside the key. There is an exception to this half court zone coverage and that's when your team is using a full court press. The full court press is explained later in this chapter under the heading, *Full Court Pressure*.

Zone Defense Setups

When using a zone defense there are different setups (ways) to divide the half court.

- **The Two-Three Zone.** This is the most popular zone defense. There are two zones near the free throw line; one out to each side of the basket (these are usually covered by quick guards). Behind them there are three more zones: one directly under the basket in the middle of the free throw lane, and one zone out to each side, covering part of the free throw lane and part of the neighboring area. Use this defense when you need good coverage out to the sides of the basket.

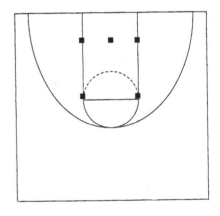

- **The Two-One-Two Zone.** In this setup there are two zones near the free throw line; one out to each side of the basket (these are usually covered by two quick guards). Behind and in between the two front zones, is a center zone in front of the basket. Your tallest player should take the center zone and be prepared to stop the progress of any opponent who enters the lane. Behind the center zone and out to the sides of the basket, are two more zones. These are usually guarded by taller players.

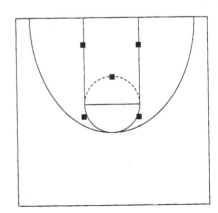

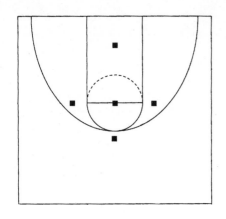

- **The One-Three-One Zone.** One zone is the central area of the backcourt, around the top of the key. Behind this zone are three zones: one covering the area on one side of the key, one covering the area on the other side of the key, and one covering the middle of the key. The last zone is the area directly under the basket.

Zone defense works best when:

- **Your opponents are faster.** If you're guarding player-to-player, and your opponent can outrun you, you won't be able to stay with him all the way to the basket. In zone defense, once the opponent leaves your zone, your teammate takes over.

- **Your opponents are taller.** If you're guarding player-to-player, a taller opponent can get his arms above yours and take a shot. In zone defense, your players will be tightly guarding the area near the basket.

Other advantages to using the zone defense are:

- **You want to keep the offense from getting an inside shot.** If you keep your zone defense tight around the key, the opponents won't be able to get inside the key, and they will have to take a longer shot.

- **Your team needs a little rest.** When you're defending player-to-player, you have to stay with your opponent and you'll get tired quicker than if you are covering a zone.

Outside the Lines

NO ZONE DEFENSE IN THE NBA!
The zone defense is not allowed in NBA games. It is allowed everywhere else, and it is a very popular defense in high school and youth basketball.

Combination Defense

Sometimes it's best to use a combination of player-to-player and zone defense. The two most popular combination defenses are the box and one, and the triangle and two.

Box and One

The *box and one* is a good combination defense if the opponents have one outstanding player, and the rest of their team is just average. The opponents will be depending on their superstar to make most of the shots. The box and one shuts down that superstar.

Four of the defenders play zone defense, each one taking a corner of the key, forming a box. The four defenders must be careful to watch the middle of the key because it will be left open in this defense.

The fifth player goes player-to-player against the opponent's superstar. This defender should be all over the superstar, trying to keep him from getting the ball. This defender needs to be in good shape, and he needs to be fast.

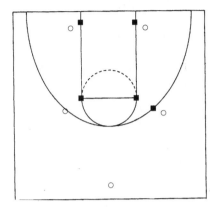

Triangle and Two

When the other team has two very good shooters, use the *triangle and two*. Three defenders form a zone around the key, and the other two defenders go player-to-player against the two good shooters.

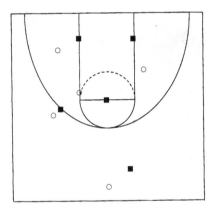

Working Your Opponent

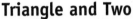

When Your Opponent Has the Ball

When guarding your opponent, always keep your body between the ball and the basket. How close you play to your opponent depends on whether or not he has his dribble left. If your opponent still has his dribble left, be careful not to get too close. If you're too close, a good head fake by the opponent, or a pick by the opponent's teammate will get you off your opponent and leave him in the clear to take a shot. Stay about three feet from your opponent so you will have room to recover from a pick or a fake and still be able to block his path.

If your opponent has already picked up his dribble, move in close to him. Follow the ball with your eyes and hands, and do everything you can to stop the opponent from getting off a pass or a shot.

7-2 DEFENSE TIGHT: The pass is only one pass away. Guard your man tight to deny him the ball. Good peripheral vision is important to keep both the ball and the man you're defending in your sights.

7-3 DEFENSE AT DISTANCE: If the ball is more than one pass away, put a little more distance between you and your man. Use peripheral vision to keep an eye on what your man is doing and what the play is doing at the same time. Always stay between your man and the basket and never lose sight of where he is.

When Your Opponent Doesn't Have the Ball

When your opponent doesn't have the ball, locate the ball. If the ball is one pass away from your opponent (close enough to get to him in one pass), move in close to keep your opponent from receiving the pass (Figure 7-2).

If your opponent is two passes away from the ball (too far away to get the ball in one pass), move off a bit (Figure 7-3). Here's why:

1. **You can guard the middle of the key.** This is an area that must be protected at all costs, because this is where the offense can get an easy shot.

2. **You can help your teammates.** If someone gets picked off their man, you might be able to guard their opponent.

3. **If you leave your player open, one of his teammates might pass to him.** Since he's two passes away, the ball will have to get past some of your teammates before it reaches him, and there might be an opportunity to steal the ball.

Outside the Lines

JUMP BLOCKS

When the jump shot was first used in basketball, it was very successful because the defenders didn't jump. Bill Russell, the Boston Celtic great, changed the game by demonstrating that a player could not only jump to block shots, but could control the game by choosing when and where to block shots. Now players regularly jump to block shots. Still, the shooter has the advantage of knowing when he will release the ball.

Working with Your Teammates

Full Court Pressure

In the *full court press,* your team keeps pressure on (guards) the offensive players in both courts (backcourt and front court) instead of just in your team's backcourt.

Use the full court press when:

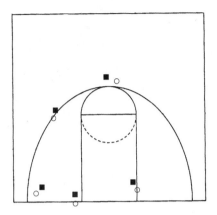

1. **Your team is in better shape.** A lot of times, the offense will dribble the ball up their backcourt slowly in order to get a rest and catch their breath. If you pressure them in their backcourt, you'll tire them out. If they're tired, they may get sloppy and your team might get a chance to steal the ball. (If the other team is in better shape than your players, don't use the full court press. Your team will tire first.)

2. **Your team is quicker.** When your players are faster, they won't have any trouble staying with the offensive players in their backcourt. (If the other team is quicker than your team, don't press them in their backcourt or they'll run right by you.)

3. **They have poor ball handlers.** If this is their weakness, try to steal the ball in their backcourt, before they move the ball into their front court and get a chance at a shot.

4. **You're behind and time is running out.** Pressing the other team in their backcourt will hurry them up and might cause them to make a mistake.

5. **They have momentum.** Sometimes teams get momentum, meaning that they are playing well, making their shots, and not making any mistakes. A full court press can help break that momentum and upset their rhythm.

Outside the Lines

THE LONE DEFENDER
According to *The Amazing Basketball Book: The First 100 Years,* in 1937 in Fairmont, West Virginia, in an intramural game, Pat McGee of St. Peter's High School found himself facing the other team, all alone. All of Pat's teammates had fouled out! The score was tied 32—all with four minutes left in the game. Pat kept the other team from scoring and he racked up three points by sinking a basket from the floor and making a foul shot.

7-4

Player-to-Player or Zone?

Just as there are two types of defense, there are two types of full court pressure: player-to-player and zone. Player-to-player defense is very simple—guard your player over the whole court. Don't let your opponent receive the ball. Play a step away from him when he's two passes from the ball.

Zone defense on the full court is a little harder because the size of your zone is bigger than when you're defending the half court. In order to make the playing field smaller, drive the offensive players toward the sideline, which will keep them from traveling in that direction.

Another strategy in the full court zone press is to double team (put two defenders on) any player who has the ball (Figure 7-4). Having two defenders on the ball handler might force him to make a bad pass.

7-4 DOUBLE TEAM: The double team is most commonly used in a full court press or when a player with the ball is in a corner. Two men trap the player with the ball, guarding him as closely as possible. As one of the defenders, your arms and hands should shadow wherever the ball is held (up, down, to the side) to block off passing lanes and the passing player's vision.

Half Court Trap

One of the rules of basketball states that once the ball crosses over the midcourt line, it is not allowed to go back. A strategy called the *half court trap* is a great way for the defense to take advantage of that rule.

Cover the ball handler, player-to player, as he nears the midcourt line. Try to force him toward the sideline. As soon as the ball carrier crosses over the midcourt line, another defender joins you so that the ball handler is trapped by you, your teammate, the sideline, and the midcourt line. Since the opponent can't go back over the midcourt line, he will be trapped, and have to pick up his dribble and pass. The pass probably won't be a good one.

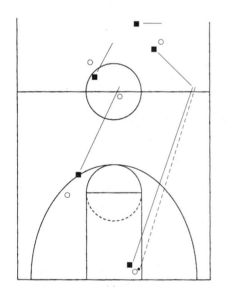

Blocking a Shot

What happens when the opponents have made it to their front court and are about to take a shot? If you're guarding the ball handler, you have three options:

1. **Be a pest.** If you can't out jump your opponent, then don't think about going for the ball. Put your hand in the shooter's face. Don't touch him, but get as close as you can. That might cause your opponent to miss his shot, and there will be a rebound. As soon the opponent shoots, turn and box him out.

2. **Stuff it.** If you are taller than the ball handler, or if you have great jumping ability, jump straight up in the air (make sure you don't jump into the shooter). Get your hand on the ball before the shooter releases it. Stop the ball and stuff (push) it back at him (Figure 7-5).

3. **Swat it away.** Instead of stuffing the ball at the shooter, you can swat (knock) it away. If you can, swat the ball toward the middle of the court.

Taking a Charge

You are not allowed to jump in front of a player who is driving toward the hoop, but you can become an obstacle in his path, and *take a charge* (let him run into you) (Figures 7-6 and 7-7). First you have to establish position by getting in front of him. Then plant your feet and stay put. If he plows into you, it's his fault, and he has committed an offensive foul. The ball is then turned over to your team.

7-5 SHOT BLOCK: Once a player goes up for a shot, it's the defensive player's job to alter his attempt in any way possible. To block a shot, jump straight up and concentrate on getting a piece of the ball. Be careful not to make contact with the shooter's body or shooting hand, or a foul will be called.

7-6 and 7-7 TAKING A CHARGE: To take a charge, position yourself in a spot that you feel is in the path of the player with the ball. Stand with the arms outstretched and feet firmly planted. (Remember, your feet can't move.) As the offensive player makes contact with you, fall back to the floor. A little acting in this defensive strategy never hurts.

Skier Squat Drill

Player-to-player defense means bending your knees and getting low to the ground, which forces your quadriceps (large muscles in the front of your legs) to do a lot of work. The skier squat will strengthen your quadriceps.

You need to work with a wall for this drill. Plant your feet about a foot from the wall. Lean your back against the wall, then slide your body down the wall until your thighs are parallel to the ground. Hold this position for up to one minute, but stop any time you feel pain. Add fifteen seconds to your time every day.

Make It Up, Play It Out

Defensive One on One

For this game you need two players, a basketball, and a half court. This game is a regular one-on-one basketball game, but you don't get any points for scoring a basket. Instead, you get a point every time you steal the ball or get the rebound. The first person to get twenty-one points is the winner.

Corners

This game teaches the players to move into the open position to receive a pass. You need four players, a basketball, and a square playing area with boundaries.

Three players are outside players—they each stand in a corner of the square. The fourth player stands in the middle of the square. The outside players may only pass along the lines of the square, not across the middle. They may only move along the lines of the square, and not cut across the middle.

The three outside players (the passers) should make sure the ball handler always has two passing options. This means that the players without the ball are constantly switching corners. For example, if the ball starts in corner one, corners two and three need to have a player in them so that the first passer has a choice to pass to either neighboring corner. In this case, corner four is empty.

If the ball is passed from corner one to corner two, the player who is in corner one stays where he is because he is still next door to the corner with the ball. But the player from corner three must run over to corner four in order to be next door to the corner with the ball, and to be open to catch a pass.

If the middle person is able to get the ball away from a passer, then the middle player trades places with the passer.

1. The basic defensive stance keeps you low to the ground and able to move around.
2. Stay close to your opponent if he has the ball, and back off from him when he is farther from the ball.
3. Player-to-player defense means that you're responsible for guarding a certain offensive player.
4. Zone defense means that you're guarding a certain area.
5. In a full court press, you put pressure on the opponent at both ends of the court.
6. Try not to foul. Force your opponent to foul you.

Glossary

Alley-oop pass—A long, high pass thrown at the level of the basket, so a teammate can jump up, get the ball, and slam dunk it into the basket.

Alternating possession—Whenever two players on opposing teams both get their hands on the ball, or cause the ball to go out of bounds, the rule of alternating possession tells the referee which team gets the ball. The rule of alternating possession means that the teams take turns getting the ball.

Backboard—The rectangular board from which   the basket is suspended.

Backcourt—Your team's backcourt is the half of the court with the basket that the other team shoots for. Your team's backcourt is the other team's front court.

Back door—When a player cuts behind a defender to get in the clear.

Bank shot—A shot where the ball is bounced off the backboard before going in the basket.

Baseball pass—A long, one-handed pass that is thrown with same motion used to throw a baseball.

Basket—The goal. The basket has a hoop (metal ring) with a net hanging from it. The hoop is attached to a backboard that is ten feet above the floor

Bounce pass—A pass in which the ball is bounced once between the passer and receiver.

Box and one—A combination defense. Four defenders play the corners of the key and the fifth defender guards the best shooter on the other team.

Box out—When a player turns his butt into the defender's stomach and moves backward in order to keep the defender from going after a rebound.

Center—A playing position. The center is usually a taller player who plays close to the basket. The center also starts the game for his team with a jump ball.

Center circle—The small circle in the middle of a basketball court. The center circle is where the game starts with a jump ball.

Chest pass—A two-handed pass that's thrown from the player's chest, directly to another player.

Coach—The coach is the team's leader. The coach teaches his players how to play the game, and plans the strategy for each game.

Combination defense—A defense that combines using zone and player-to-player defenses.

Court—The play area for a basketball game. The court used by the NBA is fifty feet wide and ninety-four feet long. In high school, the court is usually eighty-four feet long. In youth league, the court may be smaller.

Crossover—A player changes hands while dribbling and moves away from the defender toward the basket.

Cut—A sharp change of direction by a player while in motion.

Defense—When the other team has the ball, then your team is playing defense. Your team's players are the defenders, because they are defending your backcourt against the other team, who is trying to get a basket and score points.

Defensive rebound—A rebound at the basket that you're defending.

Defensive stance—The way you hold your body while you're on defense. Stay low with your knees bent, you feet wide apart, your arms out to the sides, and your head up.

Dribbling—Bouncing the ball off the floor with one hand. You may use either hand to dribble, but not both. You may switch hands while dribbling.

End line—There are two end lines, one at each end of the basketball court. A player who crosses the end line during play is out-of-bounds.

Fake—Using body language to fool your opponent.

Fast break—Moving the ball upcourt as fast as possible after a rebound.

Field goal—All successful shots are field goals, except for a free throw.

Formation—When the players are assigned certain positions on the court.

Forward—A playing position. There are two forwards on a team. They handle the ball in the front court.

Free throw—After being fouled by an opponent, a player gets one or more free throws from the free throw line. Other players are not allowed to interfere with the free throw(s).

Free throw lane—The lines on the court from the ends of the free throw line to the end line mark off an area called the free throw lane. An offensive player may not stay in the free throw lane longer than three seconds while his team has the ball in the front court.

Free throw line—A line drawn on the court that is fifteen feet out in front of the backboard.

Front court—The front court is the half of the court with the basket that your team shoots for. Your team's front court in the other team's backcourt.

Full court press—A defense strategy in which the defenders closely guard the offensive players in their backcourt as well as in the front court.

Goal—The basket.

Guard—A playing position. There are two guards on a team. The guards are usually smaller and faster players who handle the ball well. The guards usually play outside the three-point line. 2. To guard an opponent means to stay with him and make sure he can't get a shot.

Half court trap—When the ball handler is trapped between the sideline, two defenders, and the midcourt line. (Once the ball handler crosses the midcourt line, he can't take the ball back over the line.)

Handoff—A very short pass in which one player hands or flips the ball to a teammate.

Held ball—When two opponents each have their hands on the ball.

High post—The area around the foul circle. 2. A player that stays in the area around the foul circle.

Hook shot—A one-handed shot from close to the basket. The ball is thrown over the player's head in an arc toward the basket.

Hoop—The basket.

Inbound pass—After a basket is made, or after certain fouls, the ball is taken out of bounds and then must be passed back into bounds in order to start the play. When the ball is passed back into bounds, it's called an inbound pass.

Inside position—When a player is closer to the basket than his opponent.

Jump ball—The game begins with a jump ball. The tallest players from each team stand in the center of the court, inside the restraining circle. The referee tosses the ball up between the two jumpers, who leap into the air and try to bat the ball to a teammate.

Jump shot—A shot where the player jumps while shooting the ball.

Key—Another name for the free throw lane and circle.

Lay-up—A one-handed, jump shot from one side of the basket.

Low post—The area close to the basket. 2. A player that stays in the area close to the basket.

Midcourt line—The midcourt line divides the court into the front court and the backcourt.

Momentum—When a team is playing well, making their shots, and not making any mistakes, they have momentum.

NBA—National Basketball Association. NBA players are the pros (professional players).

NCAA—National Collegiate Athletic Association. This is the group that makes the rules for college basketball.

Offense—When your team has the ball, they are playing offense.

Offensive rebound—A rebound at the basket that your opponents are defending.

Officials—There are three officials at every game, two umpires and one referee. The officials make sure the rules are followed.

One-three-one zone—A setup for zone defense with one zone at the top of the key. Behind this zone are three zones: one covering the area on one side of the key, one covering the area on the other side of the key, and one covering the middle of the key. The last zone is directly under the basket.

Outlet pass—A long pass used to get the ball down the court quickly after a defensive rebound.

Out-of-bounds—Whenever a player touches the floor or any other object outside the sidelines or end lines, he is out-of-bounds.

Overhead pass—A pass thrown from over the head.

Overtime—When a game ends with a tie score, an extra time period (overtime) of three minutes is added. If the score is still tied at the end of the overtime, another overtime is added. Overtimes are added until the tie is broken.

Pass—A pass is when one player throws the ball to another player. Passing the ball is the fastest way to move it up the court.

Personal fouls—Any player who holds, pushes, hits, or trips another player commits a personal foul. When a personal foul is called, the other team gets the ball.

Pick and roll—When an offensive player blocks a teammate's defender, then rolls away from the defender toward the basket.

Pivot—When a player turns, or pivots, on one foot in order to change direction. 2. The area close to the basket where the center usually plays.

Player-to-player defense—A defense in which each defender guards a certain offensive player.

Point guard—A playing position. The point guard is usually the best ball handler on the team. The point guard does a lot of ball handling and dribbling.

Possession—When you are dribbling the ball, or when you have it in your hands, you are in possession of the ball. A team is in possession of the ball, when one of its players has the ball.

Post player—A playing position. The post player plays inside the three-point line and stays near the basket. The post player rebounds and makes power lay-ups. In the point guard system, there are two post players. In the two guard system, there is one post player.

Power lay-up—A lay-up from a standing position under the basket.

Press—When the defenders put pressure on the offensive players.

Rebound—When a shot hits the rim or the backboard and misses the basket.

Referee—An official who makes sure the rules of the game are followed.

Restraining circle—A circle in the middle of the court that contains a smaller circle, known as the center circle. One player from each team stands in the restraining circle for a jump ball to start the game.

Rocker step—When a player has the ball and rocks from one foot to the other to fake the defender and get clear.

Shoot—To throw the ball at the basket.

Shooting window—On an overhead shot, the ball is brought up to the forehead and the arms make an opening, or window, so the player can see the basket.

Sideline—There are two sidelines, one on each side of the court. A player who crosses the sideline during play is out-of-bounds.

Slam dunk—A shot where the player jumps up above the rim and slams the ball in the basket.

Spin—When the ball revolves, or spins, in the air as it is passed.

Square up— When a player turns his body toward the basket before shooting.

Strategy—A plan of action. 2. The game plan.

Stuff—To block a shot at the rim.

Swish—The sound the net makes when the ball makes passes cleanly through the basket.

Taking a charge—When a defender plants himself in front of an opponent and the opponent runs into the defender.

Technical foul—All fouls, except for personal fouls, are called technical fouls. Examples of technical fouls are: delaying the game by keeping the ball from going back into play, taking more than five time-outs, or having more than five players on the court at one time.

Three-point goal line—A large half-circle that is drawn on the floor around each basket. Any goals made from behind this line count for three points.

Three second rule—When your team has the ball in the front court, your players can't stay in the free throw lane longer than three seconds.

Traveling—A player may move the ball by passing or dribbling, but they may not walk or run while holding the ball. If they do, it's called traveling, and it's a violation.

Triangle and two—A combination defense. Three defenders form a zone around the key and two defenders go player-to-player with the other team's two best shooters.

Triple threat position—A stance that gives an offensive player the option to shoot, pass, or dribble.

Throw-in—A method of putting the ball back in play from out-of-bounds.

Turnover—Any ball-handling error that gives the ball to the other team.

Two-one-two zone—A setup for zone defense with two zones near the free throw line; one out to each side of the basket. Behind and in between the two front zones, is a center zone in front of the basket. Behind the center zone and out to the sides of the basket, are two more zones.

Two-three zone—A setup for zone defense with two zones near the free throw line; one out to each side of the basket. Behind them are three zones: one directly under the basket in the middle of the free throw lane, and one zone out to each side.

Umpire—An official that makes sure the rules of the game are followed.

Violation—When a rule is broken.

Zone defense—A defense in which each defender guards a certain area of the court.

Index